KNOW *your truth,*

SPEAK *your truth,*

LIVE *your truth*

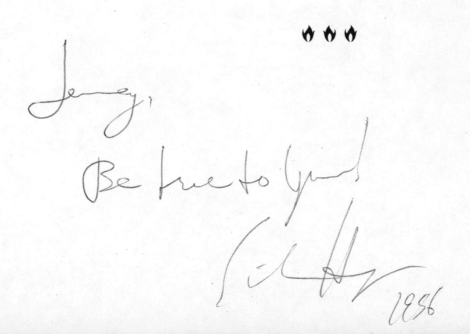

KNOW *your truth,*

SPEAK *your truth,*

LIVE *your truth*

EILEEN R. HANNEGAN, M.S.
WITH
ELIZABETH S. MACDONELL

BEYOND
WORDS
Publishing
I N C

BEYOND WORDS PUBLISHING, INC.
4443 NE Airport Road
Hillsboro, Oregon 97124-6074
503-693-8700
1-800-284-9673

EDITOR: Elizabeth S. MacDonell
DESIGN: Leigh Wells
TYPESETTING: William H. Brunson Typography Services
PROOFREADING: Marvin Moore

Printed in the United States of America
Distributed to the book trade by Publishers Group West

The corporate mission of Beyond Words Publishing, Inc.:
   Inspire to Integrity

Library of Congress Cataloging-in-Publication Data
Hannegan, Eileen R.
    Know your truth, speak your truth, live your truth / by Eileen
Hannegan.
        p.   cm.
    ISBN 1-885223-34-X (pbk.)
        1. Self-acceptance.   2. Self-evaluation.   3. Self-perception.
    I. Title
    BF575.S37H36   1996
    158'.1—dc20   96-4160
                                                                    CIP

DEDICATION

To my women's group, Supporting Your Spiritual Seasons:
Anita, Carol, Cyndie, Gayl, Peg, and Sara. For four years
of love, support, and encouragement. Thank you.

Table of Contents

~~~

Acknowledgments   IX

Introduction   XI

Part One: KNOW YOUR TRUTH   I

Chapter 1:   What Is Your Truth?   3
Chapter 2:   Finding Your Truth   5
Chapter 3:   Changing Direction   II
Chapter 4:   The Fear of Knowing Your Truth   23
Chapter 5:   Intuition: Inner Knowing   33
Chapter 6:   Practical Insights and Skills
                in Knowing Your Truth   4I

Part Two: SPEAK YOUR TRUTH   43

Chapter 7:   The Importance of Speaking Your Truth   45
Chapter 8:   Talking Versus Speaking   49
Chapter 9:   Speaking in Society   59
Chapter 10:   Speaking from Anger   65
Chapter 11:   The Fear of Speaking Your Truth   69
Chapter 12:   Inner Speaking: A Divine Resounding Whisper   77
Chapter 13:   Practical Insights and Skills
                in Speaking Your Truth   8I

Part Three: LIVE YOUR TRUTH   83

  Chapter 14: Living Your Truth   85
  Chapter 15: Being True to Your Truth   89
  Chapter 16: Being a Model for Others   93
  Chapter 17: Fear and Other Blocks   97
  Chapter 18: Inner Living: Integrating Mind,
                 Spirit, and Body   103
  Chapter 19: Living Your Truth Sexually   107
  Chapter 20: Practical Insights and Skills
                 in Living Your Truth   113

Postscript: As Your Journey of True Self Continues...   117
Recommended Readings   119

ACKNOWLEDGMENTS

A special thank you to the following people who have helped make this book possible:

Maria Chavarria, who has never wavered in her belief in me, for her faithfulness to stand in truth with compassion and power.

My dear friends Jim, Joan, Cynthia, Carol C., Claire, Norm, Dan, Patti, and Cathi, for their constant love, support, and encouragement every step of the way.

Scott Benge, who has encouraged me to keep the vision and who continued to believe in me and my work through the process of life-death-life.

Don Clarkson, who told me two years ago that I had to finish this book and that it would be "uncommonly successful—maybe a best-seller!"

Aanelies Anderson, who gave me the support and encouragement I needed when I didn't know if I could go the full distance to accomplish the goal.

Nancy Pagaduan, my guardian angel.

Cindy Black and Richard Cohn of Beyond Words Publishing, for believing in the message of this book and my ability as the messenger.

Liz MacDonell, my editor and the book's midwife, for her steadfast focus and her ability to blend the passion of the message with the structure of the book.

Bill Brunson, Marvin Moore, and Leigh Wells, for their energetic and professional efforts in turning the manuscript into a beautiful book.

And last, my deepest thanks to my daughters, Brenna and Erin, who have taught me about life, love, and truth.

INTRODUCTION

One day six years ago, Mary sat in my office for the first time, telling me her life story and of all the joys, upsets, and hurts that she had experienced. She had recently reached a point of total frustration, realizing that she had spent the last forty years trying to be a "good person" by making the other people in her life happy. But she hadn't paid much attention to herself. She now realized that this strategy had not worked—either for others or for herself. She was exhausted. She knew that she could not go back to living the way she had been, but neither did she know how to go forward.

Even though she did not know what the outcome would look like, Mary knew that she had reached a transitional crossroads—the threshold of significant change. But this knowledge brought with it tremendous fear of the unknown and uncertainty about how her spouse and other people in her life would react if she changed.

She looked at me with emptiness and a desperate need for the one answer that would make everything OK, and my heart went out to her. I had experienced similar crossroads in my own life on several occasions. I knew that she was facing the choice of life—the life of her true self, which could no longer be sacrificed and drained by being focused on the outside demands of others at the cost of her own well-being. I also knew that she had the answer deep inside her and that what she needed was direction and support to reconnect to her truth.

As she continued to stare at me, she said, "This is too much. I can never get through it all!"

I quickly responded, "Oh yes you can. It's very simple. You only need three fundamental pieces in order to chart your life transition." The words jumped out of my mouth, but I did not know where they came from. What three fundamental pieces was I talking about? My mind was blank but my inner knowing was stirred up.

Mary inched toward the edge of her chair, and life came back to her eyes. She was all ears, anxiously awaiting the information she so desperately needed.

I sat forward in my chair, too, just as eager as she to know what my inner voice would say next. As I opened my mouth, out it came! "First," I said, "you have to start discovering the truth of who you are. You have to *know your truth.*"

I went on to explain that we usually know what other people expect and want from us, but many times we are not as clear about what we need and want for ourselves until we begin to go against it and start feeling depleted. The spark in her eye told me she agreed. She was very clear about what everyone else in her life wanted from her, but aside from their happiness, she was not clear about what she wanted or needed for herself.

It was time for the second piece. Her eyes grew bigger with anticipation. Mine grew bigger with desperation. Confidently I stated, "After you get to know your truth, the next step is to bring it into existence by ... (*'What is it?'* I screamed in my head) ... by ... (*silence*) ... by *speaking your truth."* I adjusted my voice, which had gone up a few octaves in excitement, and continued, "Speaking your truth declares who you are. If you cannot speak your truth, you will not be able to activate the third piece, *living your truth."*

At this point I was on fire, telling her that "know your truth, speak your truth, live your truth" would serve as a three-part foundation to transition and transformation in both her personal and professional life. By now Mary had a smile on her face and tears in her eyes. She looked more confident, knowing that she at least had a handle on her frustration and a map to help guide her on her journey to finding her own answers by discovering and connecting to her true self. As I hugged her good-bye, I reminded her that even though the foundation pieces were simple words, her journey was in fact a challenging, lifelong process. It would take time to face the fear and to deal with old beliefs and behaviors in order to bring to life new beliefs and behaviors born out of connection to true self.

On her way out the door, Mary thanked me for throwing her a lifeline when she was deep in despair. She said, "I now see there is a way out and there is a way in. Thank you for reminding me of me. I had forgotten all about *my* truth. Now I need to discover it to make sense of my life and to bring peace and joy back into my life and work."

To this day, I'm not clear where my words came from when I spoke them to Mary, but they have never left me. The words "Know your truth, speak your truth, live your truth" have become a part of my being and have served as an activating formula for personal and spiritual growth.

And the people with whom I have shared these words have also realized significant movement forward in their personal and professional lives by working the steps of knowing, speaking, and living the truth of self. Now I would like to share them with you.

For most of the human population, as for Mary, it takes time to get to the crossroads of realization and insight. It takes time to fully realize that all the effort that has been used to deny self and to focus on outside demands throws us out of balance. It takes time to understand that being out of balance with one's self is in direct resistance to being connected to true self and to the spiritual path of wholeness. Many of us have learned the hard way that focusing the majority of our attention on outside pressures without investing in true self is unhealthy. For us, the price of depleting our emotional and physical well-being to the point of exhaustion and despair has become too high. We lose our *selves*, the unique individuals we were meant to be.

After all the hard work of trying to meet the ever-present expectations of others, a person often begins to wonder, What went wrong? How could this happen? Why am I not happy? I was doing all the right and good things to be a right and good person. It's not supposed to turn out like this. I'm confused. What about all the social and religious beliefs that have fortified these behaviors in my mind?

Ultimately, we experience an emotional crash and come to the shocking realization that our lives do not match the storybook outcomes we expected.

Many women have been willing to sacrifice their selves in order to have another person take responsibility for their lives. It seems to be easier and safer to let someone else take this responsibility—and ultimately the blame. Men, on the other hand, often take the position of "responsible protector." This role, too, promotes an outside focus without leaving room for connection to true self. Regardless of who takes what role, this arrangement usually does not have a positive outcome. Even with love, commitment, and the best of intentions, if there isn't sufficient time and attention given to individual cultivation of connection to true self, an authentic relationship with others is not possible.

In other words, the key is this: *You cannot have an authentic, healthy relationship with others until you have an authentic, healthy relationship with your true self.* A relationship with your true self creates a foundation of self-validation. It defines who you are, what your boundaries are. It allows you to interact with and nurture others without depleting yourself emotionally and physically. It is what allows you to be you—physically, mentally, emotionally, and spiritually.

You may be saying, Sounds easy—I know who I am. But do you really? Do you truly know the person inside of you—your true self? When we are asked to define ourselves, most people start by describing their careers, whether or not they are married, how many children they have, and myriad other details of their physical lives. If they are questioned again more directly, "Who *are* you and what is the purpose of your existence?" most people will find themselves speechless, their mouths hanging open and a glazed look of shock on their faces, and the resounding question, "Yeah, who *am* I?" ringing in their heads.

The true self has gotten lost—lost in the demands and the focus of others, lost in the shoulds and shouldn'ts of society and religion. Every day we feel this sense of lost self. We need to find the road back to the center, to the core of our being, to connect with the essence of self. True self!

I have written this book because of the heartbeat of passion for change and growth that I share with fellow searchers who are longing for truth and authenticity in their personal and professional lives. My hope is that this book will provide inspiration, encouragement, and practical steps to assist my fellow searchers in their pioneering efforts. On this journey of connecting to true self, the floodgates of love, wisdom, compassion, and healing will open to quench the parched dryness of the human condition.

I believe now is the time for those of us who are ready, willing, and eager for this message. I believe we have felt the longing for wholeness stirring deep inside, a longing to find the lost pieces, a longing to find the essence and reality of connecting to true self. After years of being focused on everything and everyone else in our lives, we seekers yearn to be connected to true self in order to have a life-enhancing, authentic relationship with those in our lives.

In working with thousands of men and women over the last nineteen years, I have marveled at how people struggle to meet the expectations of others at the cost of their own well-being. Yet, at the same time, I see a persistent spirit that continues to call them back to connect to true self. The intent of this book is to assist men and women in connecting with this inner calling to oneness with true self. By using the three-part foundation of *Know your truth, speak your truth, live your truth* as the road map, the people who read this book will be escorted on the journey of connecting to their true selves. My hope is that the entire human race will open to this call that comes from deep inside of us all.

May you be strong-hearted in your journey.

Part One: KNOW YOUR TRUTH

~~~~~

*To find in ourselves what makes life worth living
is risky business, for it means that once we know
we must seek. A few brave souls do look within and
are so moved by what they find that they sacrifice
whatever is necessary to bring that self into being.*

—Marsha Sinetar, *Ordinary People As Monks
and Mystics: Lifestyles for Self-Discovery*

♦

Chapter 1: WHAT IS YOUR TRUTH?

～～～～

Your truth is who you are at the core of your being. It is your pure essence—who you are without the pressures of family and society and religion telling you who to be. It is that inner voice which tells you what feels right and wrong.

Only by feeling our feelings and exploring the depth of the emotions that make up our being can we tap into the potency of true self in an authentic and effective expression in all areas of our lives. Authentic expression of true self hinges on the depth of exploration we are willing to make into the inner emotional makeup of self. It is only by delving deeply into these often uncomfortable areas that we can move through the pain of past limitations and overcome the obstacles of low self-esteem and the past rejections and betrayals of the outer world. Once we are beyond these hurdles, we can embrace the inner world of a true self that is real, healing, whole, strong, and enriching.

> Only by feeling our feelings and exploring the depth of the emotions that make up our being can we tap into the potency of true self.

Most of us have built shields of pretense over the years in order to feel safe and secure. In a sense, we have built these shields to protect ourselves from knowing the truth and have allowed *them* to become the truth. Call it a false self or a false truth. Letting go of this false self is the gateway that opens you up to knowing your truth.

In turn, knowing your truth is the first step in the discovery of true self. It does not come easily. This journey requires trust, perseverance, and courage from the depths of your soul to meet the challenges along the way and ultimately to reach the goal of connection and expression of true self. Fortunately, that courage exists deep inside all of us, waiting for us to tap into it to obtain the strength and commitment we need to achieve our goal.

I have seen in my own journey and have repeatedly observed in others that the more a person cooperates with the discovery process, the more the truth of self unfolds into all aspects of a person's life. While the process can be very difficult at times, it is absolutely necessary in order to develop the needed strength of character in the living of true self.

Ask yourself, Is this behavior/trait/belief part of my true self or has it become a part of my life based on what others have expected of me?

The journey of knowing one's truth involves many steps—paying attention to life questions, identifying the false self, facing the fear and other blocks that accompany change, and listening to your inner voice. And it may also take some time—even lots of time. But stick with it. It's worth it! It's the adventure of your life!

Chapter 2: FINDING YOUR TRUTH

To start the journey of knowing your truth, you first need to find it. Your truth can usually be found if you listen carefully and pay attention to important life questions, deal with the false truths you have created in your life in order to survive, and detach from the motivating guilt that keeps you from claiming true self.

Paying Attention to Life Questions

It surprises most people to learn that the catalysts which begin the process of knowing one's true self are often outside circumstances that call attention to what is *not* working in a person's life. When life events bring a person to the point where fulfillment can no longer be found in a career or a relationship, fundamental questions often come up and begin to point us toward the discovery of true self. Knowing your truth begins with paying attention to these events and these life questions.

When a life crisis occurs—like the breakup of a relationship, or career change, or a death—it seems as if the life we have known has been hit by a lightning bolt, crumbling the tower of protection and security that we have built for ourselves. This lightning bolt can illuminate all the aspects of our lives—good and bad—and challenge us to the core of our beliefs and behaviors. But as much as this is a shocking and sometimes terrifying experience,

Pay attention to the life questions that come to you in life crisis. They will point to the deeper needs of self.

deep down we recognize it as a wake-up call. It shakes us awake to pay attention to what we are doing with our lives.

Life questions begin to emerge, and as they emerge, they often have emotional codes attached to them that contain the information necessary to unlock the truth of self. Here are two examples:

♦ Life question: *"Why do I keep finding myself in relationships in which I am taken advantage of?"*

   Subconscious emotional code: *You might have a belief that the way you gain acceptance and love is to please other people and ask nothing in return.*

♦ Life question: *"I have spent my whole life accomplishing goals and here I am with the house, the cars, the vacations, and the financial security to prove it—and I feel empty. What happened?"*

   Subconscious emotional code: *You might have a belief that these accomplishments alone would fulfill you.*

Knowing your truth begins with life crisis and life questions.

These emotional codes may have been hidden in our subconscious for a long time, where they were virtually inaccessible—and where many of us would have preferred to leave them if they would just leave us alone. But there is no real choice in the matter once the questions emerge. By recognizing what life events developed and promoted a particular belief, we can interpret the emotional codes and prepare the way for discovering our true selves.

Identifying False Truths

To know the full range of your true self, you must discover and deal with many layers of what might be called false self, or false truth. The process is similar to peeling an onion. As you expose layer after layer of false truths, you finally reach the deepest levels that are the authentic expression of your life.

The first layer represents our roots—how we were raised and groomed by our family, society, religion, and the educational system in which we grew up. With good intent, these systems usually strive to groom people to have a high standard of beliefs and behaviors in order to be productive members of society. For most of us, performing to these standards within a tightly defined structure of externally imposed rules and regulations was rewarded with acceptance, validation, and promotion to the next level of conformity. In turn, this acceptance and validation from external sources became our guiding light. We conformed to an identity that was formulated by outside influences, and in the process, we began to drift from the truth of self with which we were born.

This is not to say that we do not need positive outside influences to help us grow and mature; indeed, to have a healthy society these outside influences are essential. The problem with the process is that in order to meet the expectations of these external regulators in our lives, we usually give up our own ability to investigate, discover, and connect inwardly for validation and acceptance of true self. It is this loss of the internal vali-

To know the full range of true self, you must deal with many layers of false self, or false truth.

dation capability and this total reliance on external sources of recognition that create our internal void and unhappiness.

As a side note, some people believe that rebellion against conformity to outside influences is the way to establish one's unique individuality. On the contrary! This approach generally misses the mark and actually takes one *farther* away from a connection to true self. While the motivation behind rebellion is to find true self, many times the rebellious person ends up connecting to the identity of rebellion as a false self and, as a result, never discovers his or her true self. The result of a rebellious identity may be new and unique, but it does not usually satisfy the longing for true self.

The next layer of false truth is the belief that true virtue lies in focusing on the needs and wants of others, putting them above those of our own. The impact of this deeply ingrained belief can be so strong that from an early age we begin forming our identity strictly according to the needs and wants of others, without regard for our personal needs and wants. In this way we block the path that can direct us to our true selves. To illustrate how and why we do this, I'll tell you about Bob. Bob's story is not unique. In fact, this was my story years ago, and I have heard it repeated thousands of times in my work over the years.

Focusing on others can block the path that directs you to true self.

Bob was a successful man who once came to see me for advice on how he could do more for the people in his life. As he sat down to talk to me, he appeared drawn and almost lifeless. He started to tell me all the things he had done in order to help his wife, such as making enough money so that she did not have to work and could stay home with the children. He had made it possible for her to go back to school by hiring a housekeeper and a cook. He was also taking care of her parents financially because they were elderly and in need, and he had gotten his stepson a good job to help him move out on his own. On top of all the things he was doing for his family, he was concerned about one of his employees and had helped him rent a house. The employee had other family problems, and Bob was trying to see how else he could help him.

He continued to talk on and on, telling me what everyone in his life needed and how he was trying to help them. Finally, I stopped him and asked, "What do you need and want?"

He replied, "I want them to be happy."

I repeated my question: "What do you want and need for you?"

His eyes filled with tears as he sat there, speechless. "I don't know," he finally whispered.

Explore what false truths in you were praised or nurtured or encouraged by outside influences.

Letting Go of False Guilt

Because we are so often focused and driven by the needs of others, we continue to push forward, trying to meet these unattainable goals, trying to satisfy the desires of everyone within our immediate network of family, friends, and co-workers. We enter into a cycle that inevitably leads to physical and emotional exhaustion. But with the expectations of others driving us, we continue to try harder and harder. If we slack off or take a breather, guilt rises up and spurs us to get back on track and continue to try to meet the ever-present expectations of others.

This feeling of guilt is the glue that keeps us focused on the needs and wants of others, holding us there and driving us onward. We believe the only way we can remain free of guilt is to continually conform to the expectations of others, forfeiting our own desires, wants, and needs in the process. This same guilt makes us believe we are inflicting pain, discomfort, or upset on others by not continually satisfying their expectations. But the truth of the matter is, this is a false guilt. You are not responsible for continually meeting the needs of everyone but you!

False guilt extracts a high price from the person who is controlled by it. It keeps chipping away at the true self until we reach either physical or emotional exhaustion (or both) and we confront it. Fortunately, just as a life crisis can, this exhaustion can warn us to start paying attention to discovering true self.

False guilt is the glue that keeps us focused on the wants of others instead of the needs of true self.

Examine how guilt motivates you.

Chapter 3: CHANGING DIRECTION

Changing direction to claim true self is motivated by knowing what your true self is *not* and accepting both the positive and negative aspects of self. By claiming these pieces, you will be well on your way to knowing your truth.

Knowing What Your True Self Is Not

The journey of knowing your truth most often begins by discovering what *isn't* working for you. Perhaps you notice you are having thoughts like "This isn't working for me no matter how hard I try" or "I just can't do this anymore!" or "There has to be another way!" These reactions point to the existence of a problem and alert you that you are experiencing a separation from true self. At this instant you may not fully realize that your life choices have caused this separation, nor do you recognize the loss of true self or the need to live authentically. But when you finally realize what is not working, the light of knowing begins to brighten.

> When you realize what is *not* working, the light of knowing your truth begins to brighten.

Once we have discovered we are moving in a harmful direction, it is natural for us to want to get back to the right way, right now! We expect to be able to instantly pick up a new pattern to live by and wipe our hands clean of the old ways—end of problem! Unfortunately, discovering our truth usually doesn't happen so easily. Indeed, for many people it can be quite terrifying, because at this point you really have only half the picture—the part of what true self is not. You still haven't figured out what the truth is or how to get to it.

What is so distressful for many people in this early stage of the journey is the realization that life as they knew it no longer works *and* that they don't have a clue how to make something new work. In many cases, too, the new desire to pay attention to the needs of true self is in direct opposition to the old pressure of expectations of others. This pull can exacerbate the turmoil and make things seem even scarier.

I have a friend who was raised in a very conventional, work-at-one-job-your-whole-life kind of family. She has recently come to the realization that she is unhappy in her career and needs to make a significant change. The only problem is that she doesn't have any idea yet what the new career will be, just the sense that she needs to make a change—and fast! In addition, she feels enormous pressure to please her family in order to retain their love. She has summoned the courage to disengage from what is not working and is taking a blind step into an unknown future. That experience alone can be terrifying for anyone; now she needs to summon up additional courage and trust in order to take the risk of significantly altering—or even losing—relationships that are important to her. Here's a similar story:

Andrea walked into my office one day, a wealthy, highly accomplished, impeccably dressed, and thoroughly confused woman. She explained that she was starting to recognize that her career and lifestyle were simply not working for her, despite all the outward indications of success. She was afraid, however, that any changes she made to alter her situation could threaten her marriage as well as her relationships with other people in her life. Her husband seemed very comfortable with her being the primary breadwinner, apparently not noticing that it was rapidly depleting her physical and emotional health or that she was becoming increasingly depressed. When she told her parents about her dilemma, they were surprised and upset with her "over-reaction," telling her that she should be grateful for having such a successful career and that she "should realize that not everyone has been as fortunate" as she. Andrea felt that her emotional and physical well-being were being seriously jeopardized, but she was the only person who seemed to realize it. She continued to doubt the reality of her situation until her medical doctor finally directed her to counseling.

As she sat in my office that day, Andrea said, "I know I need to let go of all of this if I am ever going to truly find myself. So tell me, when I let go . . . then what?"

Andrea's concern that friends and loved ones could disapprove of her choice, make her feel guilty, or even threaten to not be in her life if she decided to change her circumstances is a very real one. We all inevitably face the possibility of loss of approval when we choose to know our truth. Indeed, for many people the possibility of loss or abandonment can be terrifying to the point of causing them to forgo their efforts to discover true self—even if it kills their souls.

The first step in moving forward is accepting the possibility that your life is going to change if you change your life. Andrea realized that the image her family and colleagues had of her did not resonate deep down inside: it wasn't her true self and she knew it. But what next? One of the surest ways of changing other people's perception of you is to change your perception of yourself by embracing the positive aspects and, yes, even accepting the negative.

Ask yourself, What is not working for me?

Embracing the Positive Aspects of Self

Embracing the positive aspects of your true self awakens the hopes and dreams that accompany the new awareness. It will stretch you, causing you to see yourself in a different light. This is especially true if your family sees you in a negative or limited way and cannot accept the positive aspects of your true self as it unfolds.

For example, clients have told me over and over about how they were programmed to believe that their sibling was the intelligent one, the athletic one, or the attractive one. The message, of course, is "You're not" intelligent or athletic or attractive. Needless to say, carrying the message "You're not..." can block you from being able to embrace the talent, intelligence, looks, creativity, or anything else you do possess but have not been able to fully demonstrate.

The more you discover and become aware of your inner truth and are willing to receive it into your life, the more rapidly the healing of self into wholeness takes place. Embracing the positive aspects of self awakens the hopes and dreams that accompany awareness. By moving past the old tapes of "You're not…" and discovering and developing the skills, talents, and creativity that are the expression of your true self, eventually the positive aspects will begin embracing you. They will become a part of you because they *are* you.

Sometimes we have positive aspects of self that we are reluctant to embrace as our truth. We find ourselves feeling ashamed or embarrassed or fearful because our self-image does not match the positive picture we are uncovering. For instance, many people shrink with embarrassment when they are complimented on their skills or behaviors. These people are attempting to deflect or ignore the aspect being complimented because they have not accepted it into their lives. If we do accept the positive into our lives, we change how we see ourselves as well as how others see us. Our identity takes another step forward toward expanding to true self.

The more you discover and become aware of your inner truth and are willing to receive it into your life, the more rapidly the healing of self into wholeness takes place.

Sherry had worked a "regular" job for twenty years. And she longed for something more. Occasionally, she would say something about her yearning to her family and friends, but they didn't pay much attention. They assured her that she had a nice life and should be satisfied with her situation.

Sherry tried to ignore her longing for something more by focusing her attention elsewhere. She took comfort in attending art classes, especially calligraphy. When her instructor and other students commented on what a good calligrapher she was, however, Sherry downplayed her talent. Still, she kept taking more classes. Over time, the stirring for a change inside Sherry would not stop.

Embrace the positive
aspects of you, even if
they embarrass or
scare you.

She was drawn more and more to her calligraphy, recognizing the feeling of fulfillment and peace that it gave her. Finally, she began to realize that perhaps it was the "something more" she had been seeking—and simultaneously trying to ignore.

After considerable deliberation and internal turmoil, and much to her family and friends' dismay, Sherry finally announced her plan to quit her "regular" job and go into business for herself as a calligraphic artist. As her garage was transformed into an art studio, Sherry's heart soared even though the cost of the project made her take a deep breath. She had never done anything so extreme or anything just for herself and for what she knew was the expression of her true self.

Allow your positive
aspects to take root
and grow.

Sherry was quickly able to overcome being embarrassed by her talents. She now teaches classes in calligraphy and sells her art in local galleries. When I asked her in our final session if her life was still "regular," she laughed and said, "No way! It's much scarier and it's a lot more fun. As hard as it was—and it's still a struggle sometimes—it's the best decision I've ever made."

Accepting the Negative Aspects of Self

Sometimes we are very judgmental about the negative aspects of our selves, labeling them as unacceptable, bad, shameful, or dirty. We trick ourselves into thinking that if we don't admit or acknowledge our anger, rage, sexual needs, financial desires, addictions (alcohol/drugs/food/sex), etc., then no one will know they exist—not even us. What we fail to realize is that the aspects of self which we are trying to deny or hide are present in our lives even if we think we have them hidden or under control. Putting your head in the sand may work for a while, but over time this strategy fails to deal effectively with the situation. Ultimately these aspects of self will surface, negatively influencing our lives until we are willing to bring them into the light of truth.

Cathryn ignored the signs that her husband was having an affair with her best friend until nearly everyone else in the small town in which they lived knew it and tried to bring it to her attention. For nine years her whole life had been centered around Bryan, and now, without him, she felt worthless. The truth was too painful for her to face, so she began drowning her sorrows in the Three D's: Drinking, Dancing, and Dating. After nearly two years of hanging out in dark bars and dating men who were as lost as she was, this approach made her feel more empty and hopeless. She stopped dancing and dating but hung on tight to the drinking.

One weekend Cathryn took a trip by herself to a nearby lake. As she sat on the deck of her little motel room looking out over an early morning sunrise, she had a sudden flash of insight. "Nothing is going to get any better unless I quit drinking," she thought. "Bryan is no longer a part of my life, but I can be OK on my own. I need to sober up and get on with being me." She pondered her newfound wisdom until the sun shone bright over the lake.

Suddenly she realized she was inside the motel room, riffling through the phone book and calling an alcoholism-treatment center. As she talked to the person on the other end of the line, she heard some words that struck home within her: "There is a lot of love in this place." Cathryn hung up the phone and packed her things to go to the recovery center, saying over and over to herself, "Please, God, don't let me chicken out." She didn't.

One of the most revealing experiences Cathryn had during her treatment program was watching herself on video. She was able to observe for the first time the false self she projected outwardly in order to mask all of her feelings of hurt, anger, and despair. She realized how obvious it must be to everyone—except herself. Even though it was a harsh reality for her to face, Cathryn knew it was the start to unraveling her path to true self.

During her first year of sobriety, Cathryn had to learn how to live her life and socialize without the help of alcohol to numb her feelings. The feeling part was difficult at times, and Cathryn began to experience again all the pain, grief, and rage she had stifled for most of her life, then had drowned in alcohol. Her counselor at the treatment center had given her an exercise that helped when the waves of emotion engulfed her: Cathryn would go with the emotions for twenty minutes and allow herself to feel all of their intensity. After twenty minutes, she would wash her face, comb her hair, and leave the house to go see a friend or go shopping. This routine helped her tremendously as she kept walking through the layers of emotions that continued to come up for her.

Today, Cathryn says her toughest struggle has been overcoming self-criticism and the feeling that she was not good enough. Yet with the help of good friends, Cathryn has learned a lot about herself and others. She now has thirteen cherished years of sobriety, and she has been able to come to a place of peace and acceptance of herself and her past. She feels her greatest gift is to share who she really is in her life and to work in the recovery field.

Cathryn now boldly states, "I truly believe that everything I had to walk through forced me to embrace and forgive myself so that my true self could unfold. Today I am becoming all I was meant to be in all areas of my life. I like who I am. My insides match my outsides."

Like Cathryn's alcoholism and low self-esteem, the negative aspects of our lives cannot be ignored, even when they are uncomfortable or painful. Escaping will only increase the pressure. The pressure will not go away, and neither will the yearning for true self, once it is recognized. Dealing with the negative emotions and/or addictions that challenge us can be like wrestling a wild animal: attempting to fight it can consume you or totally defeat you. Instead of fighting it, accept that the beast exists, then ask for help in dealing with it effectively. As Alcoholics Anonymous and the myriad recovery programs that have adapted from it have taught us, the first step in dealing with inherent negatives is admitting they exist.

Believe it or not, when the negative aspects of self are addressed, they can be wonderful opportunities for a deeper discovery of true self. They call attention to areas of our lives that need and cry out for healing and wholeness. By being real, honest, and willing to discover what these aspects of our lives are directing us to recover, we step through another gateway to knowing true self.

Your negative aspects can be wonderful opportunities for a deeper discovery of true self.

Ask yourself, What negative aspects of my self am I trying to hide from myself or others?

Worksheet: KNOWING YOUR TRUTH

〰〰〰

◊ What do I know about who I am? What are my likes? Dislikes? Needs? Wants? Desires?

◊ What have I discovered that is *not* me? In other words, what habits or behaviors do I exhibit outwardly that I know don't really match what I feel inwardly?

◊ What do I know about my self that everybody knows?

◊ What do I know about my self that nobody knows?

◊ What do I wish I didn't know about my self?

◊ What do I want to know about my self?

◊ What do I most cherish about knowing my truth?

Chapter 4: THE FEAR OF KNOWING YOUR TRUTH

It takes tremendous courage and determination to embrace both the negative and positive aspects of self on the journey of knowing your truth. The block that usually stands in the way of embracing the true self is fear of change. When we make changes, lots of questions and uncertainties come to mind: What will happen if I take this risk? Will it result in a positive change? Will my friends and family stick by me if I change? Can I make it through the struggle? Many of us avoid change like the veritable plague because of fear, even though we know that this fear limits our life, stifles our creativity, and squelches the expression of true self.

What exactly do we fear? For many of us, change is akin to the death of the old way of life. When you lose or choose to walk away from a relationship, career, dream, addiction—or when you experience any big life-changing event that occurs *without you knowing what is going to take its place*—it is a death. And it's scary. An automatic alarm system gets triggered inside us and tries to convince us that only loss can occur from change. Therefore, when we face the possibility of making a change, we want a guarantee that everything's going to be OK before we take the risk.

What we need to remember is that the other side of loss is gain. The life-death-life cycle is a natural process of our universe. We need to focus not on the death of the old but rather on the new life and opportunities that lie beyond it. Death begets life. It's the law of nature.

Because the process of knowing your truth begins with discovering who you are not, it can be an exceptionally frightening experience. The combination of discovering what is not you but not yet knowing what *is* you is very much like being cast adrift in space, free-floating with no sense of attachment to anything solid. In this transitional process, it is easy to become disconcerted and frustrated. What you previously knew as your self begins to fade away, and a new set of knowns based on true self begins to emerge. As the old passes away, familiar habits and thought processes also begin to wither and die, but new ones have not yet replaced them.

Because of this paralyzing fear, many people choose to continue living a false existence. They are generally very adept at doing this, and living a false existence works for them to some degree because they manage to stay in a neutral zone, half alive and resisting the life force of true self. But living a false or a half-truth existence eventually takes its toll, both emotionally and physically. It takes a considerable amount of energy to hold back and maintain a neutral course of life. It goes against true self and drains the soul and spirit.

We think that if we keep sacrificing self long enough, things will get better. So we invest in situations that go against true self, and as a result, we deplete the soul. Our energy is being drained to maintain this façade and keep up the pretense of well-being.

In the process of knowing your truth, it is important to remember why you are on this journey: Your heart, soul, and spirit are pressing you forward into your truth so the full expression of your authenticity can be realized. You are in the process of birthing your true self.

Ask yourself, What fear is draining my energy?

Dealing with the Fear of Knowing Your Truth

The key to dealing with fear is acknowledging that you are afraid and that you are willing to deal with the fear in order to embrace the truth of you.

Next, gather support around you, particularly people who have faced their own fear and have embraced their own truth of self. Also, arrange a support system or program to deal with your addictions and/or the emotional issues that could block your progress to attain true self and your life purpose.

Here are some other guidelines for dealing with the fear of change:

◆ *Maintain your focus on the higher ground of your goal, which is reaching the other side of your fear. Try to keep your attention on the positive aspects of change instead of the negative.*

◆ *Acknowledge the concerns of well-meaning people in your life and at the same time do not get caught in their fear.*

◆ *Create a support network of friends who will escort you with encouragement, tears, and laughter through the life-death-life process on the path to wholeness.*

◆ Make fear your friend. Don't be surprised when it shows up. Embrace it.

◆ Use fear as a caution sign, not a stop sign. Fear cautions us to pay attention to crossroads in our lives. Fear allows us to consider our choices before we proceed forward.

◆ Acknowledge the fear, then let it go. Let it pass by you. You don't need to struggle with it or fight it. Of course you're afraid! You're a human being. So what else is new?

◆ Feel the fear and do it anyway. As you practice walking through the fear, surviving and having things work out, you will begin to realize that your fear is an overstated feeling—a feeling that you can in fact overcome.

◆ Break the fear down into smaller parts to be dealt with one piece at a time. Then begin by working on the first things first. It is OK to anticipate potential outcomes, but keep dealing with each small step one by one, and allow yourself to control the process.

◆ Keep the fear current. Most of the time our fear is linked with our history, which distorts and magnifies the situation. Ask yourself, Does my fear truly match the current situation, or am I just replaying old tapes and old fears?

◆ Assess the level of risk that you are at in dealing with the fear, and plan the actions you are willing to take accordingly. Once you have determined the level at which you are willing to deal with the fear, make a commitment to handle it in the best possible way, one step at a time.

Worksheet: FACING THE FEAR OF KNOWING
YOUR TRUTH

✦ Who are the support people who will assist me in facing and dealing with my fear of knowing my truth?

Name: _____ *Phone:* _____

Name: _____ *Phone:* _____

Name: _____ *Phone:* _____

Name: _____ *Phone:* _____

✦ What is my greatest fear about knowing my truth?

✦ What is the worst thing that could happen to me?

✦ What are the possible benefits of going past my fear?

✦ What is my fear of loss?

✦ What is my fear of change?

✦ What is my fear of gain?

✦ What is my level of risk at this
time?

Low   *High*

1   2   3   4   5

✦ What commitments am I willing to make in dealing with the fear of knowing my truth?

Understanding the Two Sides of Hope

When fear has had its turn controlling us, we usually try to escape to hope. The escape to hope makes us feel that we have outfoxed fear and its accompanying depression and that we have found a safe, positive hiding place in hope. But there are two sides of hope—one positive and helpful, the other negative and controlling.

The positive side of hope can be like a mountain climber's safety rope. By holding on to positive hope, we can establish enough of a foothold to continue along on our own. Holding on to positive hope—saying "I will get through this" and "Things will work out"—is a lifeline for many of us to gain true self.

However, the negative side of hope can have the opposite effect. Instead of giving us a "leg up," negative hope—using hope as a numbing drug—keeps us controlled by fear and by a continuing involvement in a situation that is in conflict with true self. Negative hope keeps us in the fear-based game of hoping things will get better, hoping things will work out if we try a little bit harder, and hoping the words we hear are true even though our experience tells us otherwise.

We groom and cultivate negative hope in the midst of even the most emotionally and physically depleting situations. It is like a drug, anesthetizing us from the pain of our fear. It dulls our senses until we become numb to true self and the reality of our situation while under its influence. Negative hope also disempowers us. It takes away our power of choice and sets us up to be controlled by the

Positive hope is a life preserver in a sea of fear.

Negative hope is a drug that anesthetizes emotional pain and fear.

situation instead of dealing with it from a position of empowerment.

Finally, negative hope catapults us into future thinking. We become detached from the present—and therefore detached from being centered in true self and spiritual source. When we think about the future, we avoid having to deal with the reality of today. We avoid the fear until a later date when we are shocked out of our delusion by a harsh dose of reality.

The sad fact is that many people run back and forth between fear and hope for most of their lives. They are trying to find shelter instead of finding the strength of true self. As a result, the real goal—the goal of being connected to true self and grounded in spiritual source—is missed.

Trusting Your True Self

It takes trust in spirit and self for you to walk through fear without attempting to escape into negative hope. With trust, you give yourself the opportunity to strengthen and maintain your connection with true self and spiritual source. This focused and present-in-the-moment existence provides the strength and power you need to deal with your fears and to handle any situation that happens in the most life-enhancing way.

Let go of hope and exchange it for faith and trust. Trust your process of life transition. Trust the life-death-life cycle of transformation. Trust your higher power. You will be present and grounded so the source of life-giving energy will support you in every situation.

Examine the two sides of hope in your life. When do you use positive hope to help you move forward? When do you use negative hope as an anesthetic?

Trust true self and spirit to walk through hope and fear.

Let go of hope and exchange it for faith and trust.

Suppose, for instance, that you are in an overly demanding relationship or work situation which is emotionally and physically depleting you. In this situation, you can "hope things will get better" or you can change your situation. The negative hope of not doing anything—maybe because you are afraid of rocking the boat—and simply waiting for it to get better on its own positions you to keep taking the abuse instead of taking the steps necessary to be true to self.

By trusting the truth of self and the process of transformation, you can set hope aside and look at the reality of the situation with clarity. You can make the choices you need to make in order to lessen the impact of the demands and to fortify your expression of true self. If need be, trust will also strengthen you to leave the situation entirely.

Ask yourself, What is it that keeps me from trusting my true self and spiritual source?

Worksheet: BREAKING THE CYCLE OF
NEGATIVE HOPE

———

◊ In what area(s) of my life do I find myself escaping to negative hope?

◊ How long have I "hoped" my life (or a certain situation) would be different?

◊ What do I hope will happen?

◊ If I don't take any steps on my own, do I believe the situation will change?

◊ If the situation does not change, how long can I live with it?

◊ What help do I need to stay in reality and not escape to negative hope?

◊ What will assist me in building trust with my true self concerning this situation?

Chapter 5: INTUITION: INNER KNOWING

Inner knowing is a deeper level of knowing that is connected to our spirit. It is our intuition, the part of us which knows without facts, experience, or other outside information that something does or doesn't feel right. It "just knows."

When inner knowing is not honored and given appropriate attention, we find ourselves overextended, distraught, and pushed too far by going against true self. When we are focused on what is expected of us instead of functioning from the inner knowing of our truth, we generally don't do a very good job of listening to our intuitive connection. When that happens, we must be prepared to deal with the consequences.

Inner knowing (or intuition, or gut feeling, or whatever you want to call it) is crucial to creating a trusting relationship with true self. But like all the other skills and awarenesses we've talked about, it takes practice. Lots of it.

It is intuition's eternal responsibility to keep us in constant communication with true self.

The first step is learning to pay attention to our intuition in the first place. With the clutter of information, input, and opinions we hear all around us, coupled with our own old tapes playing in our heads, it is sometimes hard to be in tune with the direction our inner knowing is pointing us toward.

Choose a time and quiet place where you can focus on your inner knowing. It is good to have a regular practice of time alone when you can reflect on your life and give your self room to process your feelings. Making a space for silence or retreat on a regular basis (perhaps daily or weekly) can greatly enhance the development of inner knowing. You can incorporate a meditation practice, journaling, or guided visualization tapes to help facilitate the process. For example, soak by candlelight in a hot bath or outdoor hot tub. Let yourself float weightlessly in the water and review the events of your life. Playing a meditation-music tape can also help you relax. As you review the past events, ask yourself, What do I know to be true for me? Allow the answer to come to you.

Next comes learning to trust where your inner knowing is directing you. When it sends a message that runs contrary to what your head is telling you, intuition is hard to trust. But it always proves its way true. Think back to a time when you ignored your intuition and took a job you should not have or dated a person you just didn't feel good about or invested in some real estate that just didn't sit right with you. Did you realize later, I should have listened to my intuition in the first place?

Now think back to a time when you *did* pay attention. You "went with your gut" and took a job or dated a person or invested in some property—even though your head may have told you it wasn't the logical thing to do. How did that feel? Hindsight is a good indicator of how we can come to understand and trust our inner knowing by realizing that we should have listened to our gut in the first place.

Whenever we discount or ignore our inner knowing or intuition, it generally will prove that going contrary to its direction is going contrary to true self. When we ignore the urging of intuition and go against its accurate advice and direction, we sometimes are unaware of these consequences. Fortunately, inner knowing is always willing to teach us a lesson when we go contrary to its direction of intuition. Lovingly and persistently, it directs us toward the truth of self by having us review the outcomes and results of not heeding its advice and direction.

Most people are out of touch with inner knowing because they are out of touch with its relationship with true self. By developing a relationship with true self, we can begin to know and trust our inner knowing and value the prompting of our intuition. When we become more sensitive to inner knowing through intuition by trusting its wisdom, we are able to stay centered in true self and deal accurately with whatever situation or choices have to be faced in life.

Inner knowing is the protector and champion of true self. It is intuition's eternal responsibility to keep us in constant communication with true self. By listening to and trusting your intuition, your relationship with true self will be grounded and centered in your source of strength, power, and clear direction—no matter what outside circumstances may arise to challenge your position.

Intuition is your protector and champion.

Attunement with true self is an inward journey, and it is of the utmost importance to hone the skills of communicating with this divine intuitive knowing. Here's a simple exercise for seeking inner answers to true self:

◆ *Choose an issue that is troubling you and fully define the problem.*

Example: *I feel very distant from my daughter, and I am not sure what I should or should not do in order to deal with the situation.*

◆ *Formulate a clear question about the problem that you would like to gain further insight into.*

Example: *What is the best way for me to handle this situation with my daughter?*

◆ *While in a meditative state, ask your subconscious the question. Openheartedly surrender yourself to the question without trying to manipulate or debate the answer. If you get caught in swirling emotions or if a strong emotional charge triggers fear or control issues, be willing to work through your emotions before you continue to the next step. Otherwise you will get swept away with "ego answers" instead of true self connected to spirit.*

◆ *Wait for the answer to come to you. When it does, sit with it. Don't debate it or negate it. Let it speak to you on a deeper level than words. Be one with the core you that is talking.*

Example: *"At this time, instead of talking with her about the distance between you, just love and accept her. Give her the space she needs."*

If an answer does not come after a period of time, review your inner feelings to make sure you are open to hear the answer. You may have to surrender some control in order to learn the truth. Say to yourself, "I'm willing to change. I'm willing to see differently. Please change my mind."

◆ *Give thanks when the answer comes.*

Example: *"Thank you! I really needed to hear these words of patience or I might have overreacted instead of standing in truth."*

Remember that sometimes the answer may or may not be what you wanted or had expected to hear. Many times it will surprise you because it will be the answer you knew it should be but were not willing to face. It's OK to laugh at yourself when you give thanks for an answer that exposes you by its truth.

Ask yourself, When was the last time I was in touch with my intuition? What did it tell me?

Worksheet: INNER KNOWING

⟞⟝⟞

◊ In what situation in my life did I not pay attention to my intuition/inner knowing?

◊ What warning signals did I ignore? Why?

◊ What did I learn from the experience?

◊ In what situation in my life *did* I pay attention to my intuition/inner knowing?

◊ What warning signals did I pay attention to? Why?

◊ What did I learn from this experience?

Chapter 6: PRACTICAL INSIGHTS AND SKILLS IN KNOWING YOUR TRUTH

~~~~~~

The following are practical ways to discover your true self. These skills will help you lay a strong foundation for continuing on to the next steps in the journey—speaking and living your truth.

◆ *Don't let your insights go—capture them. Knowing your truth sometimes comes in sudden ahas of insight that are provoked by thought, conversation, or experience. These insights need to be taken seriously and given immediate attention. Write them down. Don't let them go, thinking you'll remember or rediscover them later. Keep a notepad or tape recorder by your bed for middle-of-the-night insights. Keep another one with you during the day. Say your insights aloud to someone else. However you choose to do it, capture these insights and make them a part of your being. These insights will expose false self and fortify true self.*

◆ *Pay attention to motivation by guilt. When you feel guilty about something, ask yourself if the guilt really belongs to you—or if it is someone else's projection. In addition, does the guilt support or not support you in knowing your truth? If the guilt is real, take whatever steps are needed to clear up the situation as best you can. Do not be controlled by guilt.*

◆ *Embrace yourself for who you are and who you aren't. Don't fight your self. Accept the positives and the negatives as equal parts* of your self. By accepting your whole self, your attributes will increase and your weaknesses will become manageable and available for transformation. Be your own best friend.

◆ Be patient. There may be times in the process of knowing your true self when you feel like you are at the end of your rope. Perhaps you feel blocked. Perhaps you feel that moving ahead will only result in frustration and despair. At times like these, one of the best things you can do is surrender to the impasse and simply wait. Wait for the clarity from inner knowing. Wait to gain direction—and don't be surprised if the direction you receive is to remain idle. Eventually, patience teaches more patience and trust in the process. Even when you feel like you have been hung out on a limb, have faith and wait on inner knowing until strength and clarity are yours. Then move forward.

◆ Practice trusting your gut. Feel it, listen for it, ask it for insight. Pay attention when your inner knowing alerts you, and if you miss the communication (or choose to ignore it), go back and try to figure out how that happened.

◆ Practice spending time with your self. Most of us need to practice spending time with our selves in an introspective way because our society has not made much room for that part of life. Plan a regular time for sitting down with your self in silence and isolation— try a natural setting, without music or television or any other usual distractions—and cultivate a dialogue. It may seem awkward at first, but the relationship will grow stronger with time and practice. Listen carefully—you may hear some interesting things!

~~~~~~~

*Your voice is the sound track of your personality,
as revealing as a Rorschach and as individual as a
fingerprint.... The violation of the real voice often
begins, sadly, in the classroom. Children learn that
the writer's voice is different from the voice they
use every day—different and superior. Eventually,
as we grow older, something deeper and more
troubling ... makes us keep our voice inside our
heart, like a genie in a lamp. We begin to use
universal slang, psychobabble and catchphrases to
homogenize our voice, lest it seem different, inade-
quate or too revealing of our thoughts and feelings.
In Annie Hall when Woody Allen and Diane
Keaton sit down to talk for the first time, we hear
the words they speak and then the real words they're
thinking, like subtitles on the screen. One is the
societally correct voice; the second speaks from their
real selves. This is the voice we cry with, rage with
and hear in our own heads.*

It is difficult to let that voice out. But it is the only new thing you bring to the table when you write or talk; your personality—and therefore your voice—is different from that of anyone else in the world. That is why people still write books even though all the great themes were covered long ago. And it's why, timidly, tentatively, we still try to talk our own talk to the people we love.

—Anna Quindlen, *Self* magazine, May 1993

Chapter 7: THE IMPORTANCE OF SPEAKING YOUR TRUTH

━━━━━

As you travel through the journey of knowing your truth, you will begin to develop a degree of clarity in your head and a knowing in your heart that validates this truth and stirs the next stage of the process—speaking your truth— into existence.

Speaking your truth is a public declaration of your true self. It defines you and how you choose to live your life according to *your* inner truth, not someone else's needs or expectations. It is a clear declaration to yourself and others of what your commitments are in relationship to your personal and professional life.

Speak your truth into your life. Without it, you cannot live your truth.

In speaking your truth, you no longer hide in the shadow of emotional constrictions; rather, you begin advancing into the light of reality. Speaking your truth is the breath of life. It gives life to your knowingness and births your true self into reality. Only you can give or deny the words of life to true self. Only you can breathe life into its full expression.

And like knowing your truth in the first place, speaking your truth is tough work. Most of us have to overcome a lifetime of withholding our truth. We've developed a resistance to speaking our truth as a means of survival, as a way of protecting ourselves from past events and from the possibility of future rejection. Of course, the irony is that the behavior which survives as a result is precisely the one we wish to leave behind.

Only you can give the breath of life to your truth.

Even when we come to know and understand our truth, we often remain mute. The words run around inside our heads, but they don't come out: "I know I'm not happy in this relationship." "I've always known I should have been given that promotion." "I can't take this fighting any longer." Thoughts like these get caught—perhaps right on the tip of your tongue. Your heart knows you need to speak them out loud, but your head panics about all the things that might go wrong if you tell the truth.

But you know what? Things will keep going wrong only if you *don't* speak your truth. The words in your heart that declare what you have discovered about your true self need to be expressed in order to bring that knowing to life. *If you cannot speak your truth, you will not be able to live it.* Without the words of your truth, your knowing becomes dormant and lifeless. It turns into hoping instead of knowing. Without words to bring your truth to life, living your truth is not possible

To speak your truth is to find your voice of life. As Anna Quindlen says in the quote at the beginning of this section of the book, your voice is your personality. If you are without your voice—even if you know your truth—you cannot live it. You cannot be your true self. I have seen many people emotionally shrivel up, numb out, or physically die because they have no voice.

Ask yourself, What are the words in my head that I am not able to speak?

My friend Joan once told me that she received a letter from a friend telling her of a former classmate of theirs who had died after developing throat and mouth cancer. Joan told me she had

remembered how this man, Troy, had never spoken up for himself. She had often thought of him as having no voice. She herself had been struggling with speaking her truth, and she felt that the message she had gotten from this news was that Troy's voice had been taken away from him because he did not use it to claim his truth. She knew that she needed to find her voice and claim her life.

The news of Troy's death changed Joan's life forever. From that day forward she committed to speaking her truth no matter how uncomfortable or scared she might feel. Her life has significantly changed for the better since choosing to find her voice and speak her true self.

Chapter 8: TALKING VERSUS SPEAKING

Talking Society's Talk

Most of us do not find it hard to talk, especially about anything other than our selves and our truths. In fact, we can hide our truth just as easily by talking as by not speaking. What's the difference between talking and speaking? Talking is a way of producing lots of words that surround an issue without actually *speaking* the truth. The words of talking are like a camouflage, a smoke screen to hide behind so we can avoid exposing the truth of self.

Talking can be a smoke screen; speaking declares the truth.

We have been encouraged in our lives to talk but not to speak the truth. In fact, we have been strongly *discouraged* by family, spouses, society, and religion from speaking our truth, because we might upset someone. Perhaps you learned that you might be thought of as not so nice if you spoke your truth. You might even expose a lie that *everyone* has been living if you uncover your truth. Think about that as you read Esther's story.

Be aware of when you are talking versus when you are speaking your truth.

As Esther and Rob's first anniversary as a couple approached, Esther evaluated the quality of their relationship. She knew that Rob loved her, yet he could not seem to make a long-term commitment to her. She was concerned about his drinking and his party friends. Rob also continually made promises he did not keep: He said he was going to buy a car and move into a place of his own, but the words were not followed by actions. His talk was cheap. Esther had put up with Rob's late nights and irresponsibil-

ity because she loved him. But now she knew that she needed more in her relationship; she could no longer compromise her self.

After much reflection and many tears, Esther finally realized that in order to be true to her self she needed to end her relationship with Rob. She broke the news to Rob and told him that although she loved him dearly, he did not love himself. She told him that she saw and knew the beauty of who he was but that he either could not or would not let the beauty out. Ultimately, his rejection of his true self pushed her away. She could no longer allow herself to be starved for intimacy by his rejection of himself and of all that she gave to the relationship. He was not able to give her what she needed because he couldn't give it to himself.

Rob broke down and wept bitterly, agreeing with everything Esther had said. Through her tears she told him, "I can no longer help you. You are going to have to do this on your own for yourself and not for me." Rob told her that he knew he had lost her and that it was his fault. He swore he would do whatever it took to get her back. She held her ground, saying that words would not change the situation. The reality was that it would take a least a year for him to make any significant life change to establish true self, and even then, there was no guarantee that their relationship would work.

Six months later, Rob continues to give Esther monthly reports on his progress in discovering his true self. He has made advances by changing jobs, disconnecting from his party friends, and creating a stable and responsible lifestyle that enhances his self-expression. Esther is touched by Rob's progress, but she continues to be true to herself by living her truth and holding her boundaries. To fortify her stance, she has marked her calendar with the target date of one year on her own to celebrate her life and truth. She plans to be there, and she hopes that Rob will be there too.

Speaking Your Truth from Your Heart

When it is time to speak your truth, be sure it comes from your heart and not just from your head. Many times we feel safer speaking from our heads, not wanting to expose the true feelings in our tender hearts. We have learned that if we put our hearts out there, we could—and many times do—get hurt by rejection and invalidation from others.

The good news is that it is possible to extend your heart in understanding and compassion without giving your personal power away to someone else at the cost of self. By standing in the truth of self, with clarity and conviction, you are in a position to open your heart with love and compassion while still maintaining your boundaries.

Remember, speaking your truth means being right with your self and your inner conviction. It does not mean proving to anyone else that you're right. So if you position yourself in a stance that is not adversarial, then you can stand in the strength of your heart and your passion while clearly speaking your truth, whether or not anyone else agrees with you.

Let your heart speak your truth.

The truth is a very powerful force that cuts through the darkness of denial and illusion. It cuts to the core of an issue and illuminates it. Don't be surprised if some people run from the light and embrace the darkness of denial. We all know the security of denial. We have all run from the light of our own truth, and because of that we are in a position to show compassion for others when we extend the light of true self but they choose to embrace denial.

Find the voice of true self that is located in your heart. It will need to be strengthened in order to speak the words of life for yourself and others. This strengthening can be accomplished by dealing with the emotional pain that may be keeping you from speaking your truth and by embracing the self-love and acceptance that is the foundation human beings need to stand firmly in true self.

Find your heart voice by practicing the art of speaking aloud. Instead of holding imaginary conversations in your head that you plan to or wish you could say to another person, say it out loud! Some wonderful places to practice speaking out loud are in your car while driving and out in nature where no one can hear you. Get to the heart of the situation and speak it with all of your soul. Let it flow with passion from the depths of your being. In this way you will prepare yourself to speak your truth from your heart to the people in your life.

Another way to find your heart voice is to pray out loud, but not in a mimicked religious way. Let the words of truth come from your very heart and surrender to the Divine. Feel your whole being at one with the words of your truth from the heart. Many times this can invoke deep emotions that need to be released so you can get in touch with the truth and heart of the matter needing resolution.

Praying out loud is a wonderful way to get out of your intellect and into the heart of your truth.

After many years of struggle, Mara had reached her late forties with a strong connection to her truth and her spiritual work. She had finally started to see daylight after learning many hard life lessons that had brought her inner peace and a trusted wisdom. She saw her life dedicated to her spiritual path and was willing to pay whatever price was required to hold her ground.

She had a sixteen-year-old daughter from her first marriage, which had ended in divorce when the daughter, Jenna, was just a few months old. Raising a daughter as a single parent while developing her spiritual awareness was an adventurous though at times difficult job for Mara. They traveled often, living in many different places as Mara sought to find her way. She eventually remarried, and their travels continued as a threesome. They even lived in a small village in Mexico where Mara studied Native spirituality with the local people. Jenna enjoyed the good and simple life that they had in Mexico until her mother returned to the United States and divorced her stepfather. It broke Jenna's heart to lose the man she considered her father. After that divorce, Mara promised Jenna that she would not marry again until Jenna was grown and on her own because they had been through so much heartache.

Now back in the United States, Jenna was attending high school, and Mara was working hard to establish her own business and a secure home for the two of them. They enjoyed a very close and supportive relationship that had been strengthened through the hardships and struggles they had encountered together. Life was

Find your heart voice by speaking or praying out loud.

moving forward, and Mara was content to be on her own. She was focused on Jenna and living her truth. Things seemed to be going quite smoothly until Drew appeared out of the past. He was a dear friend who had known Mara and Jenna for years and had faithfully kept in touch, even when they were living in other parts of the world. This time Drew wanted to talk to Mara about the many changes in his life and to let her know that he would like to move their relationship beyond friendship.

After some months of dating, all the signs were right and Drew asked Mara to marry him. Mara was so delighted that things were going so well for everyone that she failed to remember her promise to Jenna and enthusiastically accepted his proposal. When Mara told Jenna her news, Jenna accepted it graciously at first, saying nothing of the promise made so long ago. However, as the marriage plans were being made and they began to look for a house for the three of them, Jenna grew more and more quiet. After a while, she became totally sullen and went to her room whenever Drew came to visit. When Mara or Drew asked her what was wrong, she had no answer. Jenna wanted to and tried to be happy for her mother and Drew, but the tension increased. Jenna needed to protect her heart, which had not yet recovered from the disappointments of the past losses in her life.

Mara became concerned and sat alone to listen for the inner guidance of her truth. She would ask, "What is the truth of this situation? What is the real problem?" After much contemplation the answer finally came to her. She had forgotten the promise she had made to Jenna, and even worse, she had violated it in accepting Drew's proposal. She sat there stunned, realizing the betrayal that Jenna must be feeling. Mara was torn between Jenna, Drew, and her own happiness. As she sat and wept for all of them, the words of truth kept speaking to her. She knew what she must do regardless of the outcome for herself and Drew. Without delay Mara went to Jenna and apologized for not having honored her promise. As Mara restated her promise, Jenna hugged her mom and thanked her for not forgetting about her and their relationship.

Next Mara needed to tell Drew, who was off making arrangements for their new home. She wondered if she would lose Drew over this decision, but she was hopeful he would understand and help her work through the situation. She had to stand in her true self and in the truth of the situation. For her, the foundation of life and their relationship had to be grounded in truth for all three of them in order to be nourished and supported.

Drew initially received the news with disappointment and tears, but these feelings soon shifted into understanding and accep-tance. He told Mara and Jenna that he would honor their promises and be respectful of their needs. His commitment was to both of them, and he wanted to be an important part of both of their lives in the best way he could.

Worksheet: SPEAKING YOUR TRUTH

◊ From knowing my truth, what is it that I need to speak?

◊ Who do I need to speak my truth to?

◊ What do I need to do in order to be able to speak my truth?

◊ What do I dislike about speaking my truth?

◊ What do I like most about speaking my truth?

◊ What is the most memorable time of speaking my truth?

◊ What is it that fortifies me to speak my truth?

Chapter 9: SPEAKING IN SOCIETY

————————

While I have encouraged and challenged you to speak your truth, I also feel it is important to stress that you must recognize when there are circumstances where you would be better advised *not* to publicly declare your truth. Many situations require a degree of discretion for the sake of personal safety. When these situations arise, refraining from speaking out is a viable alternative. This in no way constitutes a compromise of one's commitment to true self.

Some situations require that we not publicly declare our truth or that we think seriously before doing so.

For example, many women (and some men) face physical violence if they dare speak their truth. When someone is controlled by another person who is physically abusive, there is likely not much room in the relationship for speaking the truth; the abuser generally sees things only his (or her) way. Usually in a violent environment an escape needs to be planned in order to speak and live true self. Take the necessary steps to secure your safety before you speak. Use the telephone or write a letter to speak your truth from a safe distance. Get professional support to help you handle the situation. Use legal channels to put the abuser on notice that you are choosing life and truth.

Another situation requiring serious consideration before choosing whether or not to speak your truth involves homosexuality. Knowing, speaking, and living your truth provides an arena for freely and fully living your life. Sometimes, however, individuals in high-profile positions, such as those in the military, government, and some businesses, might be jeopardized by speaking their truth. These people must realistically evaluate and realize the potential consequences of their honesty before speaking out. I am not advocating silence on this issue; I am simply saying that it is a personal choice which, for many people, involves a heartfelt decision. Many people choose to come out of the closet every day. These individuals search their heads and hearts and know they must speak the truth of self regardless of the consequences.

A third example of a situation that requires some caution in speaking your truth is one in which you are aware that the person you are dealing with might be emotionally unstable or capable of committing suicide. This is a dramatic circumstance that needs to be taken seriously but without you being held emotionally hostage. In this case, get professional help and direction in dealing with the situation. Again, I am not advising you to remain silent (which could enable the situation at the cost of self) but rather to be aware of how to approach difficult situations most effectively.

By cautiously evaluating these situations, you can determine the cost for you to be true to self and weigh it against the cost of remaining in an environment that will not tolerate your speaking out. Many times we would prefer to keep silent and not rock the boat, but the cost may be too high a price to pay. You may realize that you must remove yourself from your current environment in order to be free to know, speak, and live your truth.

Do not be held as an emotional hostage.

Keith had struggled since he was a teenager with the thought that he might be gay. This caused him considerable distress because he wanted to live up to everyone's expectations that he would live a "normal" life. As a young adult he had become quite religious. He joined a major church and attended a religious university on a full scholarship because of his outstanding accomplishments in raising and showing top-quality livestock.

In college Keith met and married Susan, a fellow student and member of the same church. Keith felt in some ways that he "had to get married" because the pressures Susan and his church put on him were great. But in spite of his reservations, he went forward with the marriage and was hopeful that it would work out and they would live happily ever after.

Keith and Susan looked like the ideal couple in outward appearance, both displaying a continual smile wherever they went. Their involvement in church and college events was admired, as was Keith's continued national recognition as a Master Showman. Before too long, however, Keith began to feel the pressure of being in a marriage in which he had no sexual interest in or attraction for his wife. It was very upsetting to see Susan cry and continually try harder to increase her attractiveness to him, but he couldn't seem to make himself care. They were seeing a counselor, but Susan was still distraught because she was not yet pregnant. To make matters more complicated, Keith also found himself becoming attracted to another student, Paul, who was involved in the national livestock-showing circuit. Keith buried himself in his studies and the care of his livestock, and he tried to ignore the inner turmoil of his life.

The strain was becoming unbearable. Keith felt guilty that Susan was not happy, and he did not want to continue upsetting her. He cared very deeply about her and kept trying to find some way to make their relationship work. Final examinations and graduation were rapidly approaching, adding significantly to his anxiety. On top of it all, he and Paul had become lovers, and he did not want Susan or the elders of the church to know.

Eventually Keith realized he was in a position he could neither escape nor continue to ignore. He could no longer deny the truth: He was gay. And he felt trapped. He was living a lie with Susan, his church, and the college. But he also realized that everything he really valued in his life would be seriously jeopardized if he spoke the truth of self. After much soul-searching and introspection, Keith confided in the marriage counselor that he was gay. At the suggestion of the counselor, and with his help, Keith told Susan that he was gay and that it wasn't her fault the marriage wasn't working. This news ignited Susan's hurt, anger, and rage at what she saw as betrayal.

Keith was relieved that his truth was finally spoken and that he no longer had to live in denial with himself or Susan. He felt heartsick when Susan left campus and returned to her family for comfort. But the toughest part of speaking his truth still lay ahead: Due to Susan's report to the elders, Keith was expelled from the university just prior to graduation, he and all his belongings were escorted off the campus, and he was excommunicated from his church. Keith moved back to his family and informed them of what had happened. He was distraught over the impact his truth had had on Susan and his family. He had never meant to hurt anyone, but he could not hide them—or himself—from the truth.

Although his life was in tatters and he had outwardly given up virtually everything he had worked so hard to achieve, Keith knew that through his declaration of the truth he was giving life and freedom to himself. As he looks back on those life events, Keith knows that this was one of the most difficult times in his life and yet one of the most important in allowing him to begin to live his life. He is grateful that when he was put in a life situation which brought him face-to-face with his true self he was able to embrace it without bowing in to the pressure of his environment.

Is there a situation in your life that needs serious consideration before the truth can be spoken?

Chapter 10: SPEAKING FROM ANGER

I have had many clients tell me things like "I finally spoke my truth, and boy did I tell *them* where to get off!" The clients further explain how they came to the end of their rope and unloaded on the person who had pushed them too far. Even though this may have been a great opportunity to get something bothersome off their chest, it probably did not facilitate speaking the truth.

Many times it is frustration, hurt, or anger that finally pushes us to the point of having to speak a difficult truth. *Warning:* This is not the time to speak. When you reach the point of volatility, you can no longer guarantee that you will remain in control of the situation and/or your own behavior. These situations are extremely dangerous in their potential repercussions to all involved. If at all possible, wait until the volatility subsides before you speak out.

Instead of speaking immediately, I suggest you detour that frustration, hurt, and anger to a place where you can safely vent it with a trusted support person. By using the detour of a safe venting place and support person, you can receive what you need in communicating your feelings and having support in the situation. This process will also provide an environment where you can clarify what the real issue is and how you will speak your truth in a direct and respectful way, and it will allow you to center yourself before proceeding forward.

If a volatile explosion is allowed to occur, on the other hand, damage can be done to the relationship. The volatile speaking serves mainly to blow off steam and to get back at the other person to hurt him or her. Many times speaking your truth doesn't happen in these explosions even though the desire to do so is often the cause for them. You may want to speak your truth, but when the confrontation occurs, it often gets directed to a petty area of disagreement that avoids the real issues.

When we are not speaking our truth, we may choose to go along with someone else's program and deny our true selves. After a while, the denied self begins to get frustrated, hurt, and angry. It is actually starving in this scenario. True self has been starving for attention and has not been allowed expression by you or someone else in your life. Eventually these conditions may cause us to lash out, which in turn leads to conflict and argument. Until the person lashing out is ready to speak and stand behind their truth, these arguments are little more than exercises in manipulation.

The bottom line is this: Speaking your truth does *not* mean participation in an argument. It means coming from a position of centeredness and self-confidence that does not require validation or buy-in from others.

Frustration and anger are good warning signs. They tell you that you are not being true to self and that you need to pay attention and take time out before you go past the point of no return. You need to step back, ask yourself what the real issue is, and determine what you do need to say to speak your truth.

Frustration and anger can warn you that you have not been true to self.

By speaking your truth in a direct and *respectful* way—without being swayed from that posture—you will be fortified in your truth and the other person will take you seriously. When you find yourself at the point of frustration and anger, ask yourself, Why am I so angry? What are the events that have led up to this? When was it that I should have spoken up and did not? As you gather this information, look deeper. Look past what was done and not done. Ask yourself, What is it I truly need to speak?

For example, instead of fighting over the petty details of a situation, you may really need to speak your truth concerning not being listened to or appreciated. You may also have to speak the truth about being taken advantage of and how that makes you feel. Whatever the real concern, be sure you speak it from your heart of truth, not from hurt and anger.

There are times in our lives when we need to take a time-out before we speak. We can take a walk in the woods or ride a bike or even scream at the top of our lungs for a while in order to vent our frustration and anger over a situation. Once we feel calmer, we can come back in a sincere and respectful manner and speak our truth in a supportive and positive way. The other person may still not see it our way, but it is important to honor both of us with the truth in a direct and respectful approach.

Reflect on the last time you were angry and ask yourself, What was anger telling me about taking care of my true self?

Chapter 11: THE FEAR OF SPEAKING YOUR TRUTH

～～～～

For many people, one of the greatest fears in the world is speaking their truth, even though doing so could free them from many things. Free from living a lie. Free from constricting their life force. Free to be a full, vibrant human/ spirit being. In short, free to live their truth.

When fear gets in the way, it forces us to focus on the possible losses instead of the potential gains. It devours our freedom. It keeps us trapped in a role that isn't natural to us. It tells us that people will be upset and hurt if we speak our truth. It tells us that we are not nice people when we speak our truth and that if we really loved others, we wouldn't upset or hurt them with the truth. It says we should do everything we can to avoid inflicting pain, including denying our own truth to keep others happy.

But the happiness that we think we are preserving when we don't speak our truth is just an illusion. Happiness that is orchestrated by not speaking out and by pretending "everything is just fine" is actually a false and shallow pretense. When you speak your truth, this pretense of happiness will be exposed and vanish, allowing the *real* truth to come forth. Only then can authentic happiness come into your life.

It is important to recognize that while being truly honest may seem harsh at times, it is really the key to a loving relationship. The way to deal with the fear of not being a nice and loving person is to recognize that without honesty and the willingness to speak one's truth, the relationship is based on falsehood and pretense. If you can love yourself and the other person enough to speak the truth, both of you will be free to enjoy a relationship based on authentic feelings and values. Speaking your truth is not about controlling others or having them do what you want. It is about declaring how you need to live your life.

The fear of not appearing loving and kind can motivate us to take responsibility to protect another person's feelings at the expense of our own true selves. By not speaking our truth and by instead functioning from fear, we insert artificiality into the relationship. To put it bluntly, this is like using a bandage to cover a festering sore. When an outsider looks at the outer dressing, all appears well. But what's underneath is not healing, and it can eventually poison the soul of the person covering up.

You pay a high price when you are controlled by fear. You give your energy—and thus your power—to the fear by focusing on how to keep it at bay instead of using that energy to walk through the fear to give life to your self. When your energy is being drained by fear, your soul starves. This drain becomes emotionally and physically depleting and spiritually numbing. By denying your truth, you cut off nourishment to your self. Your life energy pours into a bottomless pit, with no hope of replenishment. Your energy depleted, you lose your focus and sense of direction—the very elements that are vital to keeping you on your path of living your truth.

You pay a high price when you are controlled by fear.

70

The feeling of threat that fear creates casts a gigantic shadow which is usually bigger than the actual consequences of walking through the fear and speaking your truth. Because this shadow seems so very real and very huge, many times we will back down without a struggle, allowing ourselves to be overwhelmed by our emotions. This is precisely the time when we need to take back our energy, empower ourselves, and walk through the fear. Speaking your truth is the sword that cuts through fear and makes way for life and truth to be realized.

Remember, if you can't speak your truth, you can't live your truth.

Dealing with the Fear of Speaking Your Truth

My clients are usually surprised with the simple answer I give them when they ask me, "How do I get through the fear and speak my truth?"

My simple answer? "By moving your lips."

But getting to that point takes lots and lots of dedication, practice, and courage. Believe it or not, the act of getting the truth from your heart to your head to your mouth is the hardest part. Knowing your truth in your heart and head is very different from speaking it out loud. When the truth is in your heart, it's all yours—perhaps you haven't even verbalized it to yourself yet. When it's in your head, it's still hidden from others, which means there's still no risk. But the truth is also dormant and ineffective when it's left in your head. You must move your lips and produce the words out loud to start bringing it to life.

Of course, because we aren't practiced in this area of speaking the truth of self, even when the words come out we have a hard time believing them. When you speak your truth, it will challenge your old beliefs and go against the old pictures of how you have been living your life. Speaking the truth of self challenges past history so you can create a new life based on true self. By speaking, you activate new pictures of who you know you are in truth—or perhaps some old pictures that have never been allowed to come out.

Don't be surprised if doubt and conflict come hand in hand with speaking your truth. Because of the false identity you and others have come to know, it's natural to question if what is emerging is really you or just another false self. It takes time to gain a clear sense of who you are as it unfolds. Remember, knowing your truth is a lifelong process of discovery, and it takes time to become comfortable with the truth of self.

To start practicing speaking your truth, gather people around you who will support you in the process. These support people will help you validate what you know to be true and reinforce the benefits of speaking that truth. Use your support team to act out the situation you are working on. Have one of the members play the person you need to speak to. Conduct a dialogue back and forth so you are able to practice how and what you will say in speaking your truth. The other team members can give you emotional support as well as provide feedback on how assertively, positively, and respectfully (or not) you spoke your truth.

As you practice speaking your truth to your support team, you will become clearer and stronger in your knowledge of what you need to speak. Practice will also help you develop the skills you need to speak your truth to others in your life. It will strengthen your ability to speak in real situations and fortify you emotionally.

Observe how fear controls speaking your truth.

Worksheet: FACING THE FEAR OF SPEAKING
              YOUR TRUTH

————————

◊ Who are the support people who will assist me in
  speaking my truth?

  *Name:*_____ *Phone:*_____

  *Name:*_____ *Phone:*_____

  *Name:*_____ *Phone:*_____

  *Name:*_____ *Phone:*_____

◊ What is my greatest fear about speaking my truth?

◊ Who is (are) the person(s) with whom I am most fearful of speaking my truth?

◊ What am I afraid to say in speaking my truth?

◊ What am I afraid might happen when I speak my truth?

◊ In speaking my truth, what is the possible positive outcome for my true self?

◊ What is my level of risk at this   *Low*   *High*
  time in speaking my truth?   I   2   3   4   5

◊ What is it that I need to speak?

◊ What commitments am I willing to make in dealing
  with the fear of speaking my truth?

Chapter 12: INNER SPEAKING: A DIVINE RESOUNDING WHISPER

————

In the tale, La Loba sings over the bones she has gathered. To sing means to use the soul-voice. It means to say on the breath the truth of one's power and one's need, to breathe soul over the thing that is ailing or in need of restoration. This is done by descending into the deepest mood of great love and feeling, till one's desire for relationship with the wildish Self overflows, then to speak one's soul from that frame of mind . . . this labor of finding and singing the creation hymn is a solitary work, a work carried out in the desert of the psyche.

—Clarissa Pinkola Estes,
Women Who Run with the Wolves

Being in tune with the inner speaking of spirit takes practice. Practice to know the difference between mental debates, emotional overload, and the centered speaking of spirit. The inner voice is connected to the intuitive knowing that guides us, and it sometimes comes in the form of a small yet profound voice from the innermost part of our being.

The inner voice is connected to the intuitive knowing that guides us.

Inner speaking and the inner knowing (intuition) we spoke of in Chapter 5 are in many ways one and the same. The distinction I make is that of "just knowing" versus actually hearing a voice tell you something. Many people are very aware of their intuition but never hear that inner voice. Others hear their intuition as a voice, and still others experience their inner voice only once or twice in their lives. Each of us needs to spend time getting to know and experiencing the different aspects of our inner worlds. Only then can we more clearly identify the relationship we have developed with true self.

I myself hear my inner voice with regularity, and there have been a few times when the guidance has radically changed my life. The first time my inner voice spoke to me dramatically was thirteen years ago while I was on a month-long retreat in the midst of a life crisis about my marriage. I was in great pain, desperately trying to hold on to the life I knew deep in my heart I had outgrown. On a walk through the forest at the retreat center one day, I heard a voice say, *"If you do not live the life you were called to live, there is no reason for your existence."*

I stood frozen in my tracks. The voice was so real, so clear and bold, that I turned around to see if someone else was with me. But only the trees and a nearby river were in view. Deep inside I knew (and know today) that this was the voice of the Divine. I trembled, realizing that my life as I had known it was over and that I had no other choice but to choose life.

At the close of the retreat I flew home, and my husband of sixteen years met me at the airport. He could tell immediately by the look on my face that I had something serious to say to him. With deep sadness for him and for myself, I informed him that I knew I had to leave the marriage in order to find myself. I had no idea how things would turn out, yet I knew that the inner voice had spoken the truth from the depths of my being. We had struggled in our marriage for five years; perhaps my inner knowing had to turn up the volume in order for me to finally pay attention.

The inner speaking of spirit encourages forward movement. It will also warn you if you are going against true self. Many times it can be a peaceful assurance that reminds you to trust the path of truth. Just like it is necessary to cultivate the intuitive side of your nature in order to be in tune with your true self, it is also necessary to develop the ability to listen on a level that hears the inner speaking. We can easily ignore the inner speaking and become distracted by all the outer chatter of life and the pull from outside influences. Fortunately our inner speaking is faithful and continues to call us to life and truth.

Ask yourself, Do I have an inner voice? What messages has it conveyed to me?

Chapter 13: PRACTICAL INSIGHTS AND SKILLS IN SPEAKING YOUR TRUTH

As we know, moving our lips is the most important but also the most difficult part of learning to speak true self. Here are a few practical insights and skills to help you speak your truth.

◆ *Take an assertion- or communication-skills-building class.*

◆ *Think about what you need to say. Speaking your truth is more than just casual conversation; it is a declaration. Take time to prepare yourself and to think about how you want to approach your audience.*

◆ *Practice speaking your truth by yourself or, preferably, with a support team in order to strengthen your ability to speak in an appropriate manner.*

◆ *To improve the effectiveness of your declaration of truth, write down what you need to say. You can either read your declaration out loud to your intended audience or, if they are unavailable, send it to them in written form. Either way, you are still speaking your truth.*

◆ *Remember, speaking your truth is not attacking, blaming, or manipulating another person. It is your declaration of true self.*

Part Three: LIVE YOUR TRUTH

∼∼∼∼∼∼

*Each person has a specific vocation or mission to
carry out in life. He can not be replaced nor can
his life be repeated. Everyone's task is unique.*

*Ultimately, man should not ask what the mean-
ing of his life is, but rather he must recognize that
it is he who is asked.*

*In a word, each man is questioned by life,
and he can only answer to life by answering for
his own life.*

—Viktor Frankl, *Man's Search for Meaning*

🔥 🔥 🔥

Chapter 14: LIVING YOUR TRUTH

⌇⌇⌇⌇

Living your truth is the manifestation of your truth on the physical plane, the practical acting out of what you have come to know and have put into words. In short, it is living true self.

Living your truth is born out of knowing and speaking the truth of self. Knowing your truth provides a clear direction, and speaking it activates the life energy you need to bring your truth alive. The journey of living true self will lift you out of the walled city of false self and expand your horizons in new and authentic ways.

Living true self takes a daily commitment. It is always unfolding in cycles of growth and change that continue throughout your life. With each stage of unfolding there are changes that are sometimes exhilarating and sometimes devastating. Yet, all in all, each step is necessary to bring to life the full expression of living your truth.

Living true self takes a daily commitment.

And there is work to be done as you discover true self and bring it to life. It is like tempering the steel of identity through fire and water, burning off the false aspects of the self while strengthening the pure aspects of true self. Exhausting? Yes. But the benefits are immeasurable as you gain the strength of character to withstand the pressures of life and to be true to self and personal purpose.

Unlike speaking your truth, living it requires no specific oral communication. No words are needed at this stage because your actions are far more effective in expressing both the content of your message and your conviction in it. Your whole being is speaking your truth through your life expression.

Beth had experienced considerable adversity in her life, and the cumulative effects of her struggles were beginning to become too much for her to handle. She was born with a physical disability: her arm and leg on her left side were smaller than those on her right. As a young girl, her schoolmates had teased her mercilessly, and while she had succeeded in overcoming the potential physical impact of her impairment, her mother was sure that Beth had suffered significant emotional scarring which had been repressed at the time.

As an adult, Beth worked in a clerical position in a negative work environment where neither she nor her position was given much respect. Her co-workers simply expected Beth to be there for them, and they treated her in a harsh and disrespectful way. No matter how hard she tried, her efforts were never good enough to gain the recognition she deserved. In addition, Beth cleaned the lunchroom at work in order to supplement her income. While the money helped, the work added greatly to her stress. Beth's self-esteem became seriously depleted, and her outlook on life spiraled continually downward.

When Beth first came to see me at her mother's insistence, she did not have much confidence that I could help her. She explained that she felt trapped in her current situation for several reasons. She was a single parent trying to raise a son, having left an abusive marriage several years before. She had been in her current position for twelve years, and as a result, her benefits would be hard to match in a new job. Although she hadn't had a pay raise in five years, this was the best-paying job she had ever had. She also lacked a college degree and felt that her marketability was minimal. All things considered, Beth believed that her lot was the best she could hope for.

As Beth and I talked, the pureness of her intent to do a good job and to make people happy was readily apparent to me. She was more than willing to give her heart and her power to everyone except herself—she even made sure the homeless woman who lived behind the office building had food and toiletries on a regular basis! "The first step," I told her, "is to turn your feelings inward—toward yourself. It is time to treat yourself with the care and compassion you are giving the homeless woman."

After a couple of months working with her own feelings, Beth decided to quit cleaning the lunchroom. She realized that even if she needed the money, the cost to her self-esteem was too great. In standing up for herself, Beth embarked on a journey to find true self. She was struck by the realization of how she had treated herself and how she had allowed others to treat her. As Beth moved forward in defining and declaring true self in her job, she also began to realize that she needed to move on. She needed to find a new job.

One day Beth was reading an article in the Sunday paper about a new Interpretive Center being built in a National Scenic Area. The museum was going to focus on the history of the local Native Americans and the first immigrant settlers in the area. Beth noted that the Interpretive Center was scheduled to open in a few months and that, in addition to the museum, it would also contain a gift shop. She thought to herself, "I would love to be the manager of that gift shop."

Not long after reading the article, Beth had a dream in which a Native American totem appeared. Beth felt that the dream confirmed that she was the person destined to manage the gift shop. The next morning she contacted the appropriate office. Soon thereafter, she submitted her application and began the interview process. After all the interviews were completed and the candidates had been screened, Beth was selected for the job! Her positive attitude and connection with true self had paid off.

Today, Beth's life has expanded because she lives her true self. She is recognized and appreciated for her excellent management of the gift shop and its employees, and she has had many successes there. She feels confident and her energy is buoyant. As a result of looking inward to discover and recognize her true self, Beth is embracing life and all it has to offer her.

Take a moment to ask yourself the following question: "Do I choose to live the truth of self?" Sit quietly with that question. Let it resonate throughout your being. Breathe deeply and repeat the question again: "Do I choose to live the truth of self?"

So, like Beth, just do it—just live your truth. Sounds simple, doesn't it? But it takes practice, too, just like learning to know and speak your truth. And because we are imperfect human beings, when the going gets tough, it's easy to fall back on old behaviors. But don't give up. You are breaking through years and years of old beliefs and behaviors that are contrary to your truth. Day after day, know, speak, and live your truth.

Chapter 15: BEING TRUE TO YOUR TRUTH

The real challenge of living your truth is permanently adopting actions and behaviors that validate what you are speaking. This can be a bit awkward at first because often many of us have spent years denying our truth and avoiding actions that would allow us to live it. In these situations, we must work to become used to what seems like a new reality—even though we are actually coming home to that which has been real all the time.

Living your truth is making your actions and behaviors validate what you are speaking.

The test of living your truth is having your daily life behaviors consistently show others (and yourself) that you truly mean what you say and that you say what you mean. There may be many people in your life who have heard your words before but cannot accept them as true because in the past your actions have not backed up your assertions. If anything, your inability to "walk your talk" has tended to discredit the sincerity of your message.

A good way to test whether this is happening with you is to take your words away and notice what just your actions alone are communicating to others. We are all familiar with the old adage that "actions speak louder than words." What reality are your actions speaking to those around you? Are you writing a check to cover your adult child's rent even after you said that he or she must take responsibility for it? Are you going out drinking with your buddies after work even though you promised your spouse or partner you wouldn't? Are you taking on another project when you've already told your boss that you are overloaded?

Now is the time to build on the foundation of knowing and speaking your truth. Your actions must speak for themselves. Telling your adult child that you are not going to carry his or her responsibility is not enough. You must now hold on tight to that boundary, even when it is hard to do. This sends the message, "Hear what I say in my life actions. I mean what I say."

No matter what the odds, with willingness and persistence you can resurrect the life of true self in your life. The life force of true self cannot be permanently stilled. Without question, we human beings have developed ways to shut out, numb, deny, ignore, and destroy self to avoid the journey of knowing, speaking, and living true self. But lucky for us, the law of nature and the Divine does not give up, and in spite of our resistance, it will ultimately bring us kicking and screaming back into union with true self.

My mother used to sing a lullaby with the words "We are all little lambs who have lost our way." I think these words describe our plight very well. Often we feel and act like scared and confused little lambs who will grab at anything and everything, trying to secure ourselves in our hectic and frightening world, trying to keep the wolves from our door. We may have the right idea, but we have been pointed in the wrong direction. Ours is an inward journey, and we first have to step into the darkness of the unknown inner world to get to the light of truth.

True self is your faithful companion. It is there to meet you in all phases of the unfolding, even when you don't recognize it. Subtle and persistent, it is beyond the clutter and the distractions of daily life. By relaxing, these distractions become just "stuff," and you will be able to free your self from them in order to focus your energy on connection to true self. By making time and space to sit with true self, your relationship with your core will deepen and strengthen. Being anchored to true self makes it possible to deal with this "stuff" in an effective and authentic way with the power of renewing life force.

Observe whether your actions support or deny your truth.

Living true self is integrating a deep relationship with the core you into the everyday coming and going of life, doing it authentically and with the vibrant energy of life force. It is being fully present and fully alive no matter what the outside circumstances may be. Of course, when we slide back into the clutter and distractions of stuff, we must continue to keep coming back to balance in the center with connection to true self in spirit.

When you live your truth, you reveal it to others who observe you. Friends, colleagues, even strangers will see your truth expressed positively in your daily activities. You will be a model for people wanting to take their steps in the process of transition and transformation. You will become one of the "way-showers" on the path of true self.

Many of the models we have in our lives today have nothing to do with true self. Instead, they reinforce the false fantasy of illusion and performance without the substance and character of truth. Remember the ever-smiling, perfectly coifed character that comedian Billy Crystal used to play whose response to anything bad happening around him was always, "Yes, but I look *maaahvelous*"? Of course, Crystal's character was exaggerated, but we often get a similar message in society: "Look good. No matter what, keep up a happy façade."

By contrast, as a person who lives your truth you can convey the message, "Be real. Be honest. Be authentic." By breaking the mold and living true self, you can become a positive example. You can become an invitation for others to be true to self. Living your truth inspires others and gives them permission to live their own true lives in a real, honest, and authentic way, too.

Living your truth is the gift of inspiration and encouragement that offers others the opportunity to choose true freedom and true life. All human beings long to return to

Living your truth is a
gift of inspiration and
encouragement that
offers others the
opportunity to choose
true freedom and
true life.

the core truth of self. We just haven't been encouraged or shown how to do it. That's why we need to surround ourselves with inspired individuals who are seeking true self. In this way we will have the support and encouragement we need on our journey.

Coming full circle in living true self will elevate you to the level of a focused, buoyant position that is grounded in truth and the life force of spirit. You may even feel somewhat separate from people or things that distract or hold you back from truth and life. When this happens, you can better observe and evaluate distractions from true self and have the strength and energy to move forward in living an authentic daily life. Your life expression of true self can effortlessly unfold from this vantage point, free from the entrapments that in the past may have kept you off course and detached from true self. Now your focus is clear and your energy is fully released. You are rightly positioned in living true self and personal purpose.

Ask yourself, What am
I modeling to people
in my life?

Worksheet: LIVING YOUR TRUTH

⟡ By knowing and speaking my truth, what would living my truth look like?

⟡ What skills do I need in order to live my truth?

⟡ What actions do I need to stop in order to live my truth?

⟡ What actions do I need to exercise in order to live my truth?

⟡ What practices am I willing to commit to in order to bring my truth into a body level? Some examples include massage, body movement, energy work, natural hot springs, cultural dance, relaxation/meditation, holistic health, and nature walks.

⟡ What type of grooming do I need to practice in order to reflect living my truth?

⟡ What physical-fitness activity do I need to practice to reflect living my truth? Does it need to increase, decrease, or stay the same?

Chapter 17: FEAR AND OTHER BLOCKS

As was the case when you first began knowing and speaking your truth, you may also encounter fear in living your truth. But by now you are a pro at dealing with fear and you realize that you can—and will—overcome its effects. Fear is a natural response to the new and unknown. Welcome it as a messenger of a new way of life for you. Without some sense of discomfort, nothing particularly new or exciting will develop from the journey you have chosen. Rather than shrinking away, accept the challenge and move on to your destination.

Fear can also bring confusion that can hamper your forward progress by not allowing you to see a clear direction in which to go. In confusion, it sometimes seems as if the more you struggle with it, the foggier it gets. It helps to sit with the confusion and wait for the fog to lift.

Along with a healthy dose of fear, patience and the acceptance of limitations in our lives are the other key ingredients in living true self. By exercising patience in the face of limitations, we are able to come into harmony with true self and begin to trust our spiritual path. Many times we see our limitations as keeping us from true self. It is important to learn from limitations by deepening our relationship to self. Our limitations are actually the forces we need to hone the aspects of our true self and to prepare it for full expression. It can't happen overnight, even though at times we pray that it will.

Also remember that living your truth does not mean "living happily ever after." There are many times when living true self is very painful and filled with sadness. Painful life events are opportunities to stand in the truth of self and feel the pain. By feeling the pain and being with it, true self will meet you there to bring insight and clarity. In the pain of living your truth, the wisdom of your chosen path is reinforced and validated. There has to be some pain in order to take you to a higher level of understanding and awareness in living your truth. In fact, the emotional pain of life can take you to the deepest chasm of living true self.

By going to the depths, you are then prepared to ascend to the highest points in living your truth. Strength and wisdom are gained when true self is embraced in the painful events in life. Your ascension is fueled by deep-rooted experiences that draw strength and wisdom up into your being to continue your journey in a more profound way.

I feel that one of the most important aspects of living your truth is gaining the strength and power to stand on your own authenticity, with the ability to keep an open heart in connection to self and others. Living your truth in power and compassion is an incredible energy field in relationship to spirit. This life-force energy is healing and life-giving for the transformational process of the unfolding of true self. What is really wonderful about the healing, life-giving force of true self is that it extends beyond you and will affect the other people in your life.

When limitations and other roadblocks arise in life, know that they are supposed to be there to challenge us to dig more deeply to connect to true self. These challenges also test our commitment to choose true self instead of giving in to that which is more comfortable and secure.

When limitations and other blocks arise in your life, know that they are supposed to be there to challenge you to dig more deeply to connect to true self.

Living your truth comes from within you, from the core of your being. Because it comes from inside, there are no laws that can bind it. Only you can restrict the expression of your true self by allowing outside influences to bind you. Everyone has the ability to choose whether or not they are willing to commit to the process of unfolding true self. *Willing* is a key word here, because most of the time fear and other blocks can hamper progress. If you are really willing, true self will take root, spring up, and carry you through each limiting situation.

In my own life there are plenty of times when I am not willing to go forward in living true self. At times I'm too tired, and I say to myself, "This living-your-truth thing sure is a lot of hard work. I think I'm gonna take a break." Other times fear jumps out in front of me and convinces me to put on the brakes. And let's not forget just plain being comfortable and not wanting to have things disrupted. When I find myself feeling static, for whatever reason, I start repeating to myself, "I am willing to be willing. I am willing to be willing." After a while the barriers start to give way and make room for willingness to come forth and support me through the next cycle of change.

Observe how limitations deepen your experience of true self.

What to Do About the Fear of Living Your Truth

Follow the same steps for dealing with the fear of knowing your truth as we have discussed previously. Here are a few additional tips.

◆ *Observe how your life is when you're not living your truth versus how your life is when you are living your truth. Use all your senses to feel how they differ.*

◆ *Tap into your power when you live your truth. Your power will minimize the fear.*

◆ *Assess your timing in dealing with the fear. You don't need to blast through the situation, but you don't want to go so slow that you stay in neutral. Be mindful of balance and staying grounded in spirit.*

◆ *At certain times, if you are able, expand the fear to the point where you can laugh at how ridiculous it is. This can put the fear in a better perspective and enable you to deal with it more effectively.*

◆ *Overall, respect fear as a worthy opponent and prepare yourself for the challenge.*

Worksheet: FACING THE FEAR OF LIVING
        YOUR TRUTH

〰️

◈ Who are the support people who will assist me in living my truth?

Name: _____ Phone: _____

Name: _____ Phone: _____

Name: _____ Phone: _____

Name: _____ Phone: _____

◈ What is my greatest fear about living my truth?

◈ Who is (are) the person(s) I am most fearful of seeing me live my truth?

◈ What am I afraid might happen when I live my truth?

◈ In living my truth, what are the possible positive outcomes for other people?

◈ What do I need to do in order to live my truth?

◈ What is my level of risk at this   *Low*   *High*
  time in living my truth?   1   2   3   4   5

◈ What commitments am I willing to make in dealing with the fear of living my truth?

Chapter 18: INNER LIVING: INTEGRATING MIND, SPIRIT, AND BODY

Inner living is the integration of mind, spirit, and body, creating an authentic expression of true self. Your inner living supports your outer living. Inner living of your truth is the pure essence of who you are. When we live daily life according to inner living, we experience a feeling of contentment that is not shaken by outside circumstances. This feeling is not shaken because it is grounded in truth and becomes a source of power and healing for self and others.

When you are integrated in knowing, speaking, and living truth, the unfolding of your personal and spiritual power becomes evident to you and the people in your life. Functioning from the source of truth enables you to illuminate any shadows of negative energy in your life and the lives of others who are connected to you.

The personal and spiritual power that comes from this integrated, authentic expression of true self heals by bringing the light of truth into areas of darkness. These dark areas can exist on emotional, physical, and spiritual levels. By allowing the truth to come into these areas, the life-death-life cycle can bring forth new life.

Inner living and the outer expression of living your truth are the ultimate in personal and spiritual power because they enable you to be connected to the source of your truth and the truth of the universe. No other person or outside circumstance can overpower or control you. You

Inner living and the outer expression of living your true self are the ultimate personal and spiritual you.

are on solid ground and can effectively deal with anything life presents you. You are in a partnership with your self (and your higher self), and you can enjoy the strength of authentic identity and personal power.

This power is not a negative power to be used for control over others. Rather, this power establishes your personal and spiritual strength to live your life in a full and vibrant way. It is the power of being committed in a direct, clear way so that spiritual energy is available to you for the healing of self and others. The source of power for this healing is in connecting to true self, higher self, and a higher power.

Having the balance of being anchored in the inner world in the partnership of true self and the Divine, we will experience a freedom like that of a carefree child who fully trusts that all his or her needs will be provided for. There is nothing to fear because the eternal Divine source is the foundation of our lives.

Ask yourself, How is inner living being voiced in my daily expression of living my true self?

Two weeks after his wife of twenty years asked him for a divorce, Bill found out he had a brain tumor that could kill him. He had no choice but to have emergency surgery.

When Bill awoke from his surgery, he was told that he had suffered a stroke and had lost his ability to talk and swallow. He was being fed by a tube. Bill's entire world had collapsed. He had been stripped of everything, even himself.

Recovery was long and tedious. He had to start from the beginning and learn to talk and eat all over again. Whenever he ventured out in public, people stared at his twisted and limp face.

He fought through major bouts of depression so he could move forward. In this bleak place, Bill dug deep into true self and his spiritual life.

Bill was thankful for the wonderful friends he had while he went through what seemed like an eternity on his painstaking road back to life. They encouraged him, loved him, and took him into their homes when he had nowhere to go.

Over the next three years, Bill became stronger in knowing true self and in speaking of how blessed he was as a result of what he had gone through. He started proudly walking in public and smiling at the people who stared. He knew that what had happened to him could happen to anyone, even to any of the men or women who stared at him. He realized that living true self came from within and that his outside disfigurement had forced him to embrace true self at the core of his being.

Bill feels now that he has something to offer others by telling his story and living his true self. Life and living are very precious to Bill—he's paid a high price for both. But in the process of recovery, and with the help of patience and recognition of his limitations, he has integrated his inner living and daily life in true self.

Chapter 19: LIVING YOUR TRUTH SEXUALLY

An extremely important piece of living our truth unfolds for us in our sexual identity. Of all areas of our lives, sexuality is the most shrouded with taboos, constrictions, restrictions, double standards, condemnations, and sanctions of the expression of our feminine/masculine identities. Society, politics, religion, and the educational system continually send a strong message for us to keep our sexuality under wraps.

In order to develop a healthy value system regarding our sexuality, we must journey to the deepest level of integration of true self. When we are grounded in our spiritual life and comfortable in our sexuality, we tap into an incredible healing power that not only transforms our lives but also impacts the lives of those around us.

Living your truth sexually can be possible without engaging in the act of sex, or it can be very much enhanced by the expression of sex. It is a state of being fully present as a vibrant, active human being. It is a powerful force that connects us to the life force of the earth and the universe. It is being fully alive and present.

There are many skills involved in living your truth sexually: Knowing and exercising your boundaries. Knowing when to say yes and when to say no on *your* terms. Working through the taboos like "good girls don't; bad girls do" or "sex is dirty" or "women aren't supposed to enjoy sex," and sorting them out based on your own authentic values. Avoiding the black-and-white approach to life as defined by society. Walking through the discovery process of knowing your truth so you can live your truth sexually with an open and strong heart.

When you take responsibility for your sexuality, you give your self freedom and the power of choice. You also need to accept responsibility for dealing with the results of your choices. Most of us have either shut down our sexuality or allowed others to control us sexually. Either way, we have not had the power or the skills to take responsibility for our sexuality.

It is also important to mention that when a person has been sexually traumatized in her or his life, an elaborate protection system develops, emotionally distancing us from our sexuality. While this form of protection is better than none at all, it can keep the person in survival mode and hidden from true sexual self. It effectively shields that person from further trauma yet at the same time prevents him or her from discovering a truly sexually empowered self.

When dealing with personal experiences involving sexual trauma, it is extremely important to get professional assistance in healing those wounds. Professional counselors are trained to help you build a strong foundation to gain personal power in the area of sexuality.

By knowing your truth, speaking your truth, and living your truth, you provide yourself with a strong foundation of self-validation and spiritual connection, making it possible for your sexuality to be nurtured. This strong foundation of establishing true self brings your sexuality alive.

By being nurtured in this way, the sexual sensations will begin to come alive in your body because you are present and connected to all of your senses.

When your senses become more alive, the energy and ecstasy of your sexual sensations may cause you some emotional discomfort and confusion because you are not quite sure what to do with them. It is important at this point not to shut down your sexual feelings on one extreme or to let them run wild on the other. You need to realize that you are building a foundation to empower true self. This empowerment of knowing, speaking, and living your truth defines and fortifies your life choices. You don't have to shut down sexually to protect your self, nor do you have to give your self over to someone else in order to feel free.

Living your truth sexually in a balanced way is possible by standing in the foundation of a relationship with true self first. You must first embrace your own sexuality—the lover within, the lover of true self. By loving true self first, you will gain the conviction and strength to open your heart and at the same time to set and protect your boundaries in defining your sexual identity. When you and your partner are in a healthy relationship with each of your individual selves, you can then stand as partners who honor each other in sexual expression.

Explore for yourself. Take time to walk through your sexual fears to get to the other side of sexual truth for you. Develop your value system based in your true self, in your spiritual centeredness, and in what gives you balance and wholeness in your life.

Living your truth sexually in a balanced way is possible by standing on the foundation of relationship with true self first.

Learn to dress in ways that are more "you" and that express your sexuality in a subtle or more direct way. Even dressing more artistically can be a way to express your sensual self. Dress in a way that states the truth of self in the many facets of your personality in the different areas of daily life.

Take your time to discover and explore living your truth sexually in steps that are comfortable to you. Read books, take classes, or join groups that create a safe environment in which to talk about and explore your sexuality.

Cultivate your sexuality through body movement, dance, yoga, or tai chi practices. These disciplines combine Eastern and Western ways to discover your sexuality with true self.

Most of all, however you choose to explore and practice your truth sexually, keep coming back to what you value as your experience, not what others may judge your experience to be. Your evaluation is the one that matters, and it should be in balance with all the other aspects of your life. Your sexuality is one facet of your life in the same way that your work, home life, creativity, and other areas of expression are. In total, they express the truth of you.

Your knowingness, intuition, and spirit will guide you and guard you as you discover your true self sexually. By continuing to connect to true self, the alignment will remain constant. Again, the critical point here is that you must groom your strength, power, wisdom, and skill to live your truth in a healthy, responsible way so you are fortified in the expression of your truth sexually.

Ask yourself, What fear surrounds living my truth sexually?

Worksheet: LIVING YOUR TRUTH SEXUALLY

⟡ What have I discovered about my sexual self that is different from how I was raised to view sexuality?

⟡ What is difficult about dealing with myself as a sexual being?

⟡ What do I cherish about being a sexual being?

⟡ What are the spiritual aspects of my true sexual self?

⟡ What knowledge or skills do I need in order to enhance living my truth sexually?

⟡ Do I have any sexual hang-ups, fears, or other value systems that hamper me in living my truth sexually?

Chapter 20: PRACTICAL INSIGHTS AND SKILLS
IN LIVING YOUR TRUTH

———

Coming full circle and manifesting true self by living true self is an exciting process—much like giving birth to a new you. The following insights and skills will escort you on your journey.

◆ *The ability to detach emotionally from what others may think of you is one of the most important skills required. It may still hurt, and you may still be sad that others are unable to support you in your choices, but detachment will fortify you and give you the strength to move freely in the direction of living your truth. If you are unable to work through it on your own, pursue counseling or a support group to help you gain perspective on the issues you are facing.*

◆ *It is also important to gain a variety of life skills through mentoring, education, and practice to implement the actions of living your truth. For example, ask someone who has skills and talents you would like to possess to help you develop those skills under their guidance. If you come to realize that you need more education in order to live your truth fully, then investigate what classes or degrees would best support your goal. Any one of many simple but profound life skills—such as parenting, money management, communication and assertiveness, and arts and crafts—can enhance your expression of true self.*

◆ *Look around you. Who among your network of friends and contacts can best assist you in gaining the skills or insights you need to express your true self?*

◆ *Living your truth brings with it awareness of your physical well-being and the need for having a healthy diet. Your body needs to be able to support the energy level of living true self. Having a healthy, functioning body is vital. In addition, if you are polluting your body with excess alcohol, sugar, caffeine, and/or tobacco, it will impact your balance of mind, spirit, and body. By paying attention to the signals from the body and the directions from true self, you will know what needs to be added or eliminated in order to enhance the physical aspects of living true self.*

◆ *Physical skills with your body—such as exercise, martial arts, and body movement—are also helpful in living your truth. These skills bring together your female and male energies and assist in the integration of mind, spirit, and body.*

◆ *Lastly, the prerequisite of living your truth is taking responsibility for your life. To successfully live your truth, you must have the willingness to take responsibility for your life as an adult in society. Many times I have seen men and women who want to have the freedom to live their lives their way, yet they are not willing to take responsibility for their actions. People who want to "have their cake and eat it too" will not enjoy the authenticity of living their truth.*

A Helpful Practice for Living Your Truth

When you gain the clarity of knowing true self and knowing the aspects of life that are needed to bring living true self into reality, it is time to set a clear intent of the heart's desire based on this newfound knowledge.

For example, suppose you know that your job runs contrary to your true self and you have a clear idea what a job that supports your truth would need to look like. With that clear intent of what the ideal would look like, feel like, and be like for you, you can begin to create that image in thought and in meditation as well as in conversations about it with friends. This will be most helpful in creating the pieces that in time will come together into the reality of living true self.

◆ *Set a time aside, preferably at bedtime, to visualize an aspect of living your truth. For example, see yourself in the perfect job that would support you in living your truth. Make sure that the picture you visualize is simple, like a snapshot, and feel yourself in the picture. For example, see and feel yourself in your perfect job. Don't just observe the picture—be part of it.*

◆ *If you sense any emotional resistance, have a dialogue with your subconscious in a meditative state. Deal with any emotions attached to the issue so they won't hamper or sabotage your progress.*

◆ *With your eyes closed, visualize the picture and fill it up with golden light, the energy of the universe, the life-force energy.*

◆ *When the scene is filled with the golden light, surrender it to your higher self or to the Divine. Let it be enveloped or taken up with a prayer of blessing.*

◆ *Continue to do the visualization for two weeks, then discontinue it for a few weeks and see what happens. You will notice that some things will instantly appear in your life while others will appear over a period of time.*

The importance of this practice is to create positive pictures in your subconscious that will bring the practical application of living true self into reality. The false-self existence has created false-self pictures that keep being repeated in daily life. This exercise is very helpful in assisting you to clear out old data in the subconscious in order to realize a new reality.

This exercise is also a good gauge to assist you in formalizing what you want to have in your life to live your truth as well as in bringing up emotional blocks that need to be removed in order to move forward in the fullness of true self.

Postscript: AS YOUR JOURNEY OF
          TRUE SELF CONTINUES...

Always remember that you are a unique and special person whose life purpose is constantly unfolding. With great enthusiasm and joy, the universe is waiting for you to fully and authentically express the truth of you.

Be thankful for all that you have discovered and experienced of your true self thus far, and cherish the inner connection to the Divine Source that guides you.

Rejoice in how everything has been prepared in your life to bring you into relationship with true self and personal purpose. And be assured that no matter what life events you may encounter along the way, your strength and courage is waiting deep inside you, ready to be accessed.

Open your heart to yourself to know, speak, and live your truth. Then extend that open and strong heart to the other people in your life.

Surround yourself with fellow travelers along the Journey to True Self.

Most of all, enjoy the greatest adventure of your life—discovering True Self!

RECOMMENDED READINGS

Allenbaugh, Eric. *Wake-up Calls: You Don't Have to Sleep Through Your Life, Love, or Career!* New York: Simon & Schuster, Fireside, 1994.

Anand, Margo. *The Art of Sexual Ecstasy.* Los Angeles: Putnam Publishing, Jeremy P. Tarcher, 1991.

Anderson, Sherry Ruth, and Patricia Hopkins. *The Feminine Face of God: The Unfolding of the Sacred in Women.* New York: Bantam Books, 1992.

Blum, Ralph. *The Book of Runes: A Handbook for the Use of an Ancient Oracle.* New York: St. Martin's Press, 1984.

Borysenko, Joan. *Guilt Is the Teacher, Love Is the Lesson: A Book to Heal You, Heart and Soul.* New York: Warner Books, 1990.

De Angelis, Barbara. *Real Moments.* New York: Bantam Doubleday Dell, Delacorte Press, 1994.

Estes, Clarissa Pinkola. *Women Who Run with the Wolves.* New York: Ballantine Books, 1992.

Fox, Matthew. *The Reinvention of Work: A New Vision of Livelihood for Our Time.* San Francisco: HarperSanFrancisco, 1995.

Hendricks, Gay, and Kathlyn Hendricks. *Centering and the Art of Intimacy Handbook: A New Psychology of Close Relationships.* New York: Simon & Schuster, Fireside, 1992.

Hendricks, Gay, and Kathlyn Hendricks. *Conscious Loving: The Journey to Co-Commitment*. New York: Bantam Books, 1992.

Hoodwink, Shepherd. *Loving from Your Soul: Creating Powerful Relationships*. New York: Summerjoy, 1995.

Lawlor, Robert. *Earth Honoring: The New Male Sexuality*. Rochester, Vt.: Inner Traditions, 1989.

Moore, Thomas. *Care of the Soul: A Guide for Cultivating Depth and Sacredness in Everyday Life*. New York: HarperPerennial, 1991.

Patent, Arnold. *You Can Have It All*. Hillsboro, Ore.: Beyond Words Publishing, 1995.

Sinetar, Marsha. *Ordinary People As Monks and Mystics: Lifestyles for Self-Discovery*. Mahwah, N.J.: Paulist Press, 1986.

Welwood, John. *Journey of the Heart: Intimate Relationship and the Path of Love*. New York: HarperPerennial, 1991.

Whitfield, Charles. *Boundaries and Relationships: Knowing, Protecting, and Enjoying the Self*. Deerfield Beach, Fla.: Health Communications, 1993.

Wilde, Stuart. *The Quickening*. Carson, Calif.: Hay House, 1988.

Wing, R. L. *The Illustrated I Ching*. New York: Doubleday, 1982.

OTHER BOOKS FROM
BEYOND WORDS PUBLISHING, INC.

THE WOMAN'S BOOK OF CREATIVITY

Author: C Diane Ealy, $12.95 softcover

Creativity works differently in women and men, and women are most creative when they tap into the process that is unique to their own nature—a holistic, "spiraling" approach. The book is a self-help manual, both inspirational and practical, for igniting female creative fire. Ealy encourages women to acknowledge their own creativity, often in achievements they take for granted. She also gives a wealth of suggestions and exercises to enable women to recognize their own creative power and to access it consistently and effectively. Ealy holds a doctorate in behavioral science and consults with individuals and corporations on creativity.

NURTURING SPIRITUALITY IN CHILDREN

Author: Peggy D. Jenkins, $10.95 softcover

Children who develop a healthy balance of mind and spirit enter adulthood with higher self-esteem, better able to respond to life's challenges. This book offers scores of simple and thought-provoking lessons that parents can teach to their children in less than ten minutes at a time. Using items easily found around the house, each lesson provides a valuable message for children to take into their days and into their lives. The lessons are easy to prepare and understand, and each parent can alter the lessons to fit their own spiritual beliefs. The activities are adaptable for children from preschool to high school ages.

THE BOOK OF GODDESSES

Author/illustrator: Kris Waldherr

Introduction: Linda Schierse Leonard, Ph.D., $17.95 hardcover

This beautifully illustrated book introduces readers of all ages to twenty-six goddesses and heroines from cultures around the world. In the descriptions of these archetypal women, the author weaves a picture of the beauty, individuality, and unique strength which are the birthright of every girl and woman. Beautiful to look at and inspiring to read, this book is a stunning gift for goddess-lovers of all ages.

YOU CAN HAVE IT ALL

Author: Arnold M. Patent, $16.95 hardcover

Joy, peace, abundance—these gifts of the Universe are available to each of us whenever we choose to play the real game of life: the game of mutual support. *You Can Have It All* is a guidebook that shows us how to move beyond our beliefs in struggle and shortage, open our hearts, and enjoy a life of true ecstasy. Arnold Patent first self-published *You Can Have It All* in 1984, and it became a classic with over 200,000 copies in print. This revised and expanded edition reflects his greater understanding of the principles and offers practical suggestions as well as simple exercises for improving the quality of our lives.

HOME SWEETER HOME:
CREATING A HAVEN OF SIMPLICITY AND SPIRIT

Author: Jann Mitchell; Foreword: Jack Canfield, $12.95 softcover

We search the world for spirituality and peace—only to discover that happiness and satisfaction are not found "out there" in the world but right here, in our houses and in our hearts. Award-winning journalist and author Jann Mitchell offers creative insights and suggestions for making our home life more nurturing, spiritual, and rewarding for ourselves, our families, and our friends.

LETTERS FROM THE LIGHT:
AN AFTERLIFE JOURNAL FROM THE SELF-LIGHTED WORLD
Author: Elsa Barker; Editor: Kathy Hart, $12.95 hardcover

In the early part of this century, a woman begins a process of "automatic writing." It is as though someone takes over her hand and writes the document. Days later she finds out that the man has died thousands of miles away, and she is now serving as a conduit as he tells of life after death through her. His message: There is nothing to fear in death, and the life after this one is similar in many ways to the one we already know, even though we will be much more able to recognize our freedom. Readers of the book, originally published in 1914, invariably concur that the book removed from them the fear of dying.

WHEN MONEY IS NOT ENOUGH: FULFILLMENT IN WORK
Author: Eileen R. Hannegan, M.S., $10.95 softcover

When personality clashes and ego battles predominate in the workplace, no amount of money in the world is enough to justify continued employment. In an age when Americans spend more than half their waking hours either at work or performing a function related to work, it is important that the workplace be a healthy community rather than a chaotic battleground. *When Money Is Not Enough* offers the premise that work can indeed enhance our lives as well as pay the bills. The book is neither pro-employer nor pro-employee in its approach. Instead, it encourages increasing interdependency among all staff members to create a healthy work environment. Author Eileen R. Hannegan, M.S., says that approaching the workplace as a community or healthy family is the key to resolving work-related problems.

To order or to request a catalog, contact:

BEYOND WORDS PUBLISHING, INC.

4443 NE Airport Road

Hillsboro, OR 97124-6074

503-693-8700 or 1-800-284-9673

BEYOND WORDS PUBLISHING, INC.

~~~~~~

OUR CORPORATE MISSION:

Inspire to Integrity

OUR DECLARED VALUES:

We give to all of life as life has given us.

We honor all relationships.

Trust and stewardship are integral to fulfilling dreams.

Collaboration is essential to create miracles.

Creativity and aesthetics nourish the soul.

Unlimited thinking is fundamental.

Living your passion is vital.

Joy and humor open our hearts to growth.

It is important to remind ourselves of love.